Praise for *The Profitable Consultant*

"The number-one complaint my customers have is, 'I need more business!' Why? They don't have a great system, best practices, or a methodology for it; or at least not one specifically designed for consultants and coaches. *The Profitable Consultant* provides a system, a methodology to get more business and faster—if you are a consultant/coach. Most importantly, Jay introduces the powerful psychology every consultant, coach, and expert needs to break through and become a six-figure earner or go from six to seven figures! Do yourself a favor and adopt these concepts. It just might be the best business investment you ever make—period!"

—Mike Koenigs
Founder/CEO, Traffic Geyser

"Jay Niblick has cracked the code when it comes to growing your consulting practice. His method to attract more clients is both simple and amazingly effective. As I read this book, I had one 'aha' moment after another. If you want more clients and more time to do what you love, study this book and put Jay's methods to use. It will change your business—and your life."

—Noah St. John
Bestselling author of
The Secret Code of Success

"Having worked with thousands of coaches and consultants, it's heartbreaking how many never achieve success because they never figure out how to generate profits. In *The Profitable Consultant*, Jay reveals a fascinating but simple strategy to be yourself, enjoy the process, and still dominate your market at will. The first time I saw Jay's work, I immediately realized its sheer power and brilliance. It provides the missing piece that I've never seen anyone else reveal. That's why we now make his work a mandatory part of all our training programs for coaches, consultants, professionals, and entrepreneurs. If you're looking for ways to grow your practice, stop searching—this book is the answer!"

—Greg Habstritt
Founder and President,
SimpleWealth Inc.

"It's about time someone stepped up and took on the conventional way consultants have been taught to grow and sell and turned that on its head. *The Profitable Consultant* challenges you to be you and simply communicate what you do and how you do it, making the 'hard sell' not required. Instead of teaching you how to change yourself to become a great salesperson, Jay does not want to change you; he just wants to enhance you and the way you do business."

—Philip McKernan,
International bestselling author,
speaker, and President at
Philip McKernan Inc.

THE
PROFITABLE
CONSULTANT

THE
PROFITABLE
CONSULTANT

STARTING, GROWING, AND SELLING YOUR EXPERTISE

JAY NIBLICK

WILEY

Cover design: Courtesy of Art Direction Book Company

Cover design: Chris Wallace

Library of Congress Cataloging-in-Publication Data:
Niblick, Jay, 1968-
  The Profitable Consultant: Starting, Growing, and Selling Your Expertise/Jay Niblick.
    pages cm.
    Includes index.
    ISBN: 978-1-118-55313-8 (cloth)
    ISBN: 978-1-118-61627-7 (ebk)
    ISBN: 978-1-118-61637-6 (ebk)
    ISBN: 978-1-118-61638-3 (ebk)
  1. Consulting firms. 2.   New business enterprises.   I. Title.
    HD69.C6N53 2013
    001–dc23   2012048299

Printed in the United States of America

10 9 8 7 6 5 4 3 2 1

Contents

Foreword

SALES AND MARKETING CAN BE uncomfortable for professional business consultants and executive coaches. I've known many coaches who want to be *above* promoting or selling their services. They believe that their work should speak for itself and that marketing and promotion—selling—is demeaning.

Maybe they don't want to be associated with those pushy or annoying people that so often garner the title salesperson. Perhaps they don't want their clients to think of them as one of these distasteful people. Possibly they see self-promotion as a reflection of professional or personal deficit.

Whatever the case may be, it holds them back. One of the things that I frequently tell people when they ask me for advice about how to get a job in consulting is: "You have to sell yourself. You have to develop the [You] Brand." Most people aren't really salespeople. You still must sell; the trick is to do it in such a way that you are not seen as a salesperson—and that's where people need significant help.

The Profitable Consultant will give you that help. Taking traditional beliefs about how best to grow a practice and generate revenue, and turning them completely upside down, Jay Niblick rewrites the business development playbook for the consulting and coaching industry.

We're in a different field than most other professions. What we need isn't conventional business development techniques; it's a new methodology specifically designed for us—independent business consultants and coaches—and that's exactly what Jay gives us in *The Profitable Consultant*!

So, stop struggling to grow your practice and pick up this book—you will be glad you did!

—Marshall Goldsmith
New York Times and million-copy bestselling author of *MOJO* and *What Got You Here Won't Get You There*

Acknowledgments

THIS BOOK IS DEDICATED TO all those consultants around the globe who have so graciously and generously shared their best practices with me, who have put their faith in me, and who have contributed so much more than just professionally to my life. Thank you!

And to my parents, who inspired the courage to "Go boldly in the direction of my dreams"; my sisters, who supported me; and to my wonderful Melanie, Zach, Baker, and Joe, who so bravely suffered the pains of living with an entrepreneur—bless you!

Introduction

WELCOME TO THE GREATEST PROFESSION in the world. I'm talking about being an independent management consultant, an incredibly exciting and rewarding career that can also be an exceptionally lucrative one, if done correctly.

It's what I call a *brain job*. Peter Drucker would call it a knowledge worker's profession, in line with his description of a world changing from an economy of laborers to one of thinkers. Consider it becoming a free agent in an entire economy of free agents. In this career you get to take all that wonderful knowledge and experience you've developed in your professional management career and turn them into a dream job.

What other career allows you to incur almost zero overhead, work a majority of your time from home (yes, even in pajamas), spend all the time you want with your loved ones, and control exactly what work you do, and for whom?

It's no wonder that the occupation of management consultant is the single fastest-growing job in the entire country right now. According to the US Bureau of Labor Statistics, this occupation is growing at 84 percent, nearly double that of the next closest job title. From those who have been laid off to those who no longer wish to allow someone else to control their entire lives, people around the world are taking this leap.

Don't let this statistic scare you, however. There is still *plenty* of room to grow. What statistics like these do mean, though, is that this

1

isn't the same industry it was 20 years ago. Gone are the early prospector days where all one had to do was hang out a shingle, call himself or herself a consultant, and take an ad hoc approach to building their practice. Those who plan on succeeding today and staying for the long haul must differentiate themselves and step up their game.

My job in these pages is to help you do just that. I will help you reduce the number of mistakes you will make (I said reduce, mind you) and give you the wisdom and experience of thousands of other consultants who have gone before you and thrived. I know a little bit about doing that myself.

In 1998 I founded a consulting firm called Innermetrix Incorporated with my partner Damon Kohler. Originally it was just me doing consulting, with Damon handling all the technology. Today Innermetrix is an international firm with over 750 consultants in 23 countries helping tens of thousands of companies and hundreds of thousands of their employees.

The biggest benefit of working with all of these consultants and corporations has been the learning. Far more than thoughts from a single consultant, this book holds the wisdom of the very best in our profession. You will learn at the feet of many hypersuccessful consultant brothers and sisters who made their mistakes so you don't have to.

If you want to build a profitable business today, you can't just sit back and wait for business to come to you. And you can't just read this book and gain understanding of the practice of consulting. You must learn to apply these lessons. The effort you put into *practicing* the understanding I will give you in these pages is the key.

As the subtitle states, you have the expertise. That is *not* something I'm going to be able to help you with. If you're considering becoming a consultant, the presumption is that you've spent a good portion of your lifetime honing your business expertise in whatever industry or field you're in. While you bring that expertise, my job is to make you an expert in how to grow a profitable consulting practice.

These solutions have been field-tested and battle-proven. They work for all types of consultants and in all the different business cultures I've worked in as well. Through my training and certification programs I've conducted from New York to Johannesburg, Sydney to Hong Kong, and all over Europe and the United States, I've taught over 1,750 independent management consultants the same lessons contained in this book.

Even though, according to the US Bureau of Labor Statistics, 65 percent of all new start-ups fail to survive past the five-year mark, of those 1,750 consultants I've trained, 95 percent of them have survived past that same five-year mark and are profitable. Some of these consultants consistently achieve seven-figure revenue year after year, and the majority maintains healthy six-figure incomes steadily—even in the current economy! I know these lessons work, and I'm excited about helping you add your name to this list!

Welcome aboard—and now let's go build your profitable practice! For additional learning and resources on all of the lessons in this book, visit www.TheProfitableConsultant.com.

1

Is Consulting Even Right for Me?

Why Choose Management Consulting as a Career?

The career of management consultant is one of the most envied roles a person can be lucky enough to play. That title, however, is somewhat of a catchall, thrown about by people who provide a wide range of services (accountants, lawyers, strategic planning, HR, operations, etc.). For the most part professionals employed in this field provide outsourced services to organizations in need of whatever specialty that consultant provides.

For our purposes we need to differentiate between three main types of consulting firms: large diversified organizations, medium-sized management consultancies, and boutique firms.

The large diversified firms are represented by the likes of McKinsey & Company, Booz Allen, PWC, and KPMG. Mid-sized consultancies, while smaller than the large international firms, can still employ hundreds of people, and provide broad services similar to those of the large diversified firms. Then there are the boutique firms, typically having only one independent consultant and offering a more specialized suite of services or specialties. It is this last category of consultancy—the independents—that this entire book will focus on.

Typically an independent management consultant is someone who:

- Works for themselves, or possibly as part of a very small group.
- Works from home, or has a small office.
- Provides services/solutions to small to medium-sized businesses.

What is it that makes this career so coveted? The following four broad categories summarize the main reasons.

1. **Freedom/Flexibility.** As an independent consultant you are completely in control of your own destiny. Many people get into this career specifically because they are tired of working for someone else, or because they were laid off and looking to take control over their career. As an independent consultant you decide when you

work, whom you work with, and what you provide. For myself, the benefit of being able to attend one of my son's school plays, or simply to have a date with my wife in the middle of the week, is an incredible benefit. I worked for a Fortune 100 company for many years and the freedom I enjoy now far exceeds that rat race!

2. **Earnings potential.** Working for someone else typically means you work hard to make someone else rich. Sure, you can enjoy a significant salary, but the bulk of the earnings flows not to the workers but rather to the owners. As an independent management consultant you are the owner, and all the profits flow to you. Among independent management consultants we see the complete gamut of earnings. In our own network we have consultants who earn as little as $45,000 a year (by choice, mind you), and as many as 10 who earn over $1,000,000 a year. Of course, the higher levels of income don't happen overnight, so if you're expecting to get rich quick . . . well, you get the picture.

3. **Control.** One of the greatest aspects of this career is that you control what you provide and whom you provide it to. If you choose not to work with the idiotic owner of XYZ Corp, you don't have to. As the owner you get to cherry pick only those clients whom you want to work with, think you can do the most for, or enjoy working with the most. In a later chapter I'll show you how firing undesirable clients is actually a key growth tool.

4. **Fit.** Several years back I commissioned a research study that examined 197,000 workers across 23 countries over a seven-year period. The findings empirically proved that the most successful people (in any career or at any level) were those who were the most authentic to their natural talents, passions, and skills. Suffice it to say that most roles professionals find themselves taking, in corporations, aren't customized to fit personal natural talents. As an independent management consultant you alone will craft a role that is a significantly better fit for you.

What Does a Management Consultant Do?

Management consulting is the practice of helping organizations improve their overall condition, typically through analyzing existing problems, diagnosing causes, and then developing a plan for improvement or remediation. The most common reasons management consultants are brought in are:

- To provide an expertise or capability not currently possessed by the organization internally.
- To be an objective third party to legitimate existing beliefs by senior management.
- To provide political safety where decisions are difficult or run the risk of damaging existing executives' reputations.
- To bring best practices from across an industry.

While the primary objective of any good management consultant should be to improve the client's overall condition, there are multiple functions or roles a consultant may fill to achieve that objective. Another way to view the work of a management consultant is to understand the specific purpose they fulfill. There are eight fairly universally accepted roles as defined by Dr. Arthur Turner, a Professor of Organizational Behavior at Harvard Business School.

Those eight purposes are (see Figure 1.1):

1. Provide information to a client.
2. Provide a solution to a given problem.
3. Diagnose existing problem.
4. Provide recommendations.
5. Implement solutions.
6. Build consensus.
7. Facilitate client learning.
8. Improve overall organizational effectiveness.

Note: As a general rule, the higher up the hierarchy you go—the greater your value proposition (and financial worth) is to the client.

These eight purposes act as building blocks, with a foundation and ultimately a peak. They grow in complexity, value and, profitability. Let's go deeper into each one.

1. **Providing information to a client.** Often a consultant is brought in simply to help a client find information they either don't know where to find or cannot interpret practically. Many times this deals

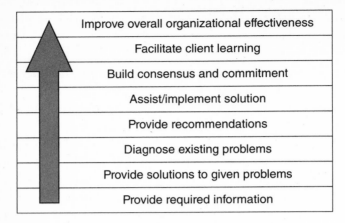

Figure 1.1 The Hierarchy of Consulting Purpose

Source: Adapted from Arthur N. Turner's "Consulting Is More Than Giving Advice," *Harvard Business Review* (1982).

with the consultant's expertise and involves historical information, expert knowledge, or current research. This type of consulting occupies the bottom level of this hierarchy because it is the least specific, most general in nature, and much closer to data analysis than true consulting. Most truly profitable consultants don't provide value in this purpose very often.

2. **Providing a solution to a given problem.** The keyword here is "given," which denotes that the client has already decided what the problem is and simply needs an expert to deliver their predetermined solutions. Simply put, this level of consulting is the hired-gun level. The danger at this level lies in tying your name and brand to work that may or may not be effective. The key question is, "Have they diagnosed the true problem and cause correctly?" In other words, you run the risk of delivering excellent training, but on something that isn't the real cause of the problem. Only if you are certain that the client has indeed accurately diagnosed the problem and the solution is valid, then is it okay to deliver it. Remember, a good consultant always makes sure they are working to improve the client's overall condition, not just to get paid.

3. **Diagnosing an existing problem.** At this level you partner with the client to identify the symptoms, define the actual problem, and then accurately diagnose the true cause of the problem. This is the ideal

first level of interaction with any client. Analogous to the physician, no consultant should ever engage without first being sure of the real cause of the problem. Otherwise they risk committing consultative malpractice. In my opinion this is the single most valuable step and, as such, it is the most valuable purpose to begin with.

4. **Provide recommendations.** At this level you help the client determine the best course of action to correct a problem, which is now accurately diagnosed. This is where consultative sales are truly made. This is the number one path to becoming the person who actually delivers the solution. In this role you have the most influence, you are able to craft a solution that best serves the client as well as you. By this I mean a recommendation that doesn't just tell them what to do to fix the problem, but one that involves your help in delivering it.

5. **Assist/implement solutions.** As the title suggests, your purpose here is to actually help deliver the solutions. Whether you're assisting the client in implementing your solution, or actually implementing it yourself, the outcome should be the same (i.e., collaborating to improve the client's overall condition). In some cases you will need to deliver the solution because it relies on expertise or skills the client doesn't possess. In other cases when the client does possess the ability, you will play more of a supervisory role.

6. **Build consensus and commitment.** No matter how grand, accurate, and easily implementable your recommendations may be, if the people affected by it fail to buy in to the solution, it will fail. Building consensus is of paramount importance to any project. All too often consultants fail to take into consideration all those who need to be on board with the recommendations. A key part of your role as consultant should always be to make sure you manage consensus building throughout the entire company. I think of Henry Ford's famous statement in matters like this, "Whether you think you can or can not, you're probably right." If you want to achieve a positive outcome, ensuring everyone is on board, and believing they *can*, is your responsibility.

7. **Facilitating client learning.** The purpose here is to leave behind knowledge the client didn't possess before you arrived. Sometimes this is more a matter of ancillary learning through experience, as the client should be involved in every aspect of your work. However,

the smart—and profitable—consultant makes this a dedicated objective and charges the client handsomely for transferring such knowledge. Of course, it's up to you to decide if you want to impart such knowledge to your clients or keep it all for yourself so they need you every time. I cover this in greater depth in Chapter 5 where I talk about the "Do it. Teach it. Support it" model (DTS), but keeping all the knowledge and training to yourself runs the following risks.

○ Each time the client needs additional training they have to decide if they want to go back outside of the organization, which creates a point where they may decide to go with someone else instead of you.

○ When faced with having to pay higher fees to bring in an outside source, many clients (especially after they have experienced your solution once or twice) mistakenly believe they know what it takes to deliver that training, so they do it on their own. More often than not this doesn't work because they are playing "monkey see, monkey do," rather than having been properly trained.

○ If you tie yourself to hours worked you limit your profitability. Every time you deliver training you are taking yourself off the market. If you do this right, you can teach the client to do the process themselves, and still get paid.

8. **Improving organizational effectiveness.** This should be the over-arching goal of any consultative work. As such, it should be the purpose or role you strive to reach with any client negotiation. There may be times where you are filling another role on this list, but all other roles should be in service of this objective. In short, the poor consultant may be happy to play a bit part in the overall play that is the client's condition, but the truly profitable consultant makes sure he or she gets the starring role! The most profitable consultants deliver their greatest value by serving in this capacity.

Types of Practice Mind-Sets

Not all consultants share the same mind-set when it comes to why they start their business. For some it's a second full-time career, but not one they intend to spend 20 years building. For others it's a part-time gig where they love the work but don't want to spend 80 hours a week doing it. Still for others it's about building what will become the pinnacle of their professional career and the primary means of supporting themselves and their family. Knowing which type of business you want to build is important.

When it comes to consulting or coaching practices, there are four kinds of practices:

1. **The Hobbyist Practice.** This is a practice that is more a hobby than a real business. Like a hobby, there is less of a strategic plan in place, fewer hours are worked, and the overall approach is more casual.

2. **The Sustenance Practice.** This is a practice that is normally meant to be a primary revenue generator, but isn't. It sustains itself, but barely. There isn't enough revenue to reinvest into the business, shoestring budgets rule the day, and often the consultant finds more month than money.

3. **The Plateau Practice.** This is a practice that is a full-time business for the consultant, and has grown through the start-up phase to moderate or even significant revenue, but then it plateaus and refuses to grow past a certain point regardless of effort, tactics, or reason.

4. **The Legacy Practice.** This is a practice that has become a true business with significant revenue and sustainable positive growth. This level of practice has developed either its own intellectual property, or a substantial enough book of business (often both) that it has a realistic exit strategy.

In this book I'm speaking to those who desire to achieve legacy standing, with the end goal of becoming a full-time, profitable, self-sustaining business that generates significant wealth and has the potential to either live on after the founder leaves or be sold for a profit.

If your goal is to run a hobbyist practice these lessons will work for you too, but you will want to consider adjusting the frequencies of work I prescribe. If you're currently running a sustenance practice these lessons hold the potential to significantly increase your revenue and elevate your practice to the legacy status. And, if you're currently running a plateau practice, I will show you how to grow past the limitations that currently restrict your growth and break your current revenue ceiling.

Trends in Management Consulting

Management consulting, as an industry, is globally a $366 billion market (see Figure 1.2). As a business service, consulting remains somewhat cyclical and is linked to the overall economic situation.

The majority of independent consultants primarily serve the small to medium-sized business market (SMB/SME). This makes up 95 percent of all businesses in the United States, with similar percentiles in most developed countries. That equals approximately 29.44 million SMB organizations with 52.6 million employees and represents 50 percent of the global GDP of $70 trillion. Some consultants also do work with very large Fortune 1000–sized companies as well, but the revenue sweet spot is with the small to medium-sized organizations that constitute most of the world's organizational business.

With companies downsizing and laying employees off, the opportunities lie in organizations that have thinned their ranks and then come across a need for expertise they no longer possess. It is far cheaper for these organizations to bring an outside consultant in than it is to pay for a full-time employee with benefits and entitlements.

Another reason why the SMB market is so ideal is that, unlike very large organizations, the consultant typically deals directly with the owner, or top executive. Because of this there is less bureaucracy or delay and greater influence and results.

Category	Revenues
Global Consulting Total	$366 Billion
Management Consulting	$148.4 Billion
HR Consulting	$12.2 Billion
Financial Consulting	$9.7 Billion
Sales/Marketing Consulting	$9.7 Billion
IT Consulting	$1.5 Billion

Figure 1.2 Global Consulting Revenues

Hiring outside consultants is also on the rise. Multiple polls show a growing trend of executives in the SMB space who decide to bring outside consultants in as a cost effective way to get the resource they need.

Risks of Independent Consulting

There are risks associated with starting any business, consulting or otherwise. Statistically, as I said in the introduction, nearly 65 percent of new businesses are gone within five years of starting and nearly two-thirds are gone within a decade. Consulting businesses aren't immune to these same statistics.

Outside of the statistical failure rates, there are unique risks associated with becoming an independent management consultant. Some specific challenges you will face include the following three.

1. **Isolation.** Most consultants work by themselves. They are called "independent" for a reason. The typical profile of a successful consultant is one that enjoys interacting with others; but, while interacting with prospects and customers is the biggest solution to the problem of feeling alone, it is an unavoidable fact that even with a busy schedule you will still be working by yourself much of the time.

2. **Self-management/accountability.** Most people fail to truly appreciate the potential danger of working for themselves, in regard to having to be completely accountable to themselves. It can become a very slippery slope to start your business without a structured (or accountable) job description. Even if you think you're disciplined, I highly recommend some sort of outside accountability partner (e.g., an external coach). Such a coach is normally another independent consultant such as yourself, but with specific training and experience as an executive coach. We have a list of them on our corporate website (www.innermetrix.com).

3. **Do-everything syndrome.** As the center of your solar system and life-blood of your business, it is incredibly tempting for most entrepreneurs to get caught in what I call the "do-everything syndrome." Simply put, you acquire this disease slowly as you take on every facet of responsibility in your fledgling business.

It's just so damn easy to do it all. As you start out it just makes sense to take on all responsibilities. However, as you grow, you have to ensure that your role doesn't become that of CEO, CFO, COO, VP of Sales, Chief Cook and Bottle Washer. To help you with this, in a later chapter is my "CEO Bucket List" exercise. It's very effective and I invite you to steal it from this book and use it with your own clients wherever applicable.

In the end, the risks of opening an independent business consulting firm are not very much different from those of opening any new small business. The greatest variable in your success is you! You will always need to stay vigilant and make sure that you're putting in the hours and work needed to ensure your own success. If you were to come to training with my company you would see a sign in the training room that reads, "The enemy thanks you for NOT giving 100 percent today!"

This message is something I looked at every day in one of my special operations training programs way back when, and it helps convey a couple of key points. First, your competition is your enemy. Viewing the competition as such is a damn good thing. The moment you fail to show up—the second you slack off and leave the smallest opening—your competition will cut in like an aggressive New York City taxi driver. They will take any opening you give them, so it's up to you to show up every day . . . 100 percent!

The good news is that you are the most powerful risk reducer in this equation—no one else.

What Experience Is Needed?

The issue of experience is very much a question that directly relates to the type of consulting you intend to offer. If you come from a 20-year background in management in the banking industry, you probably wouldn't want to provide consulting services in lean manufacturing.

Basically, there are four broad categories of experience needed to succeed as an independent consultant.

1. **Solution-specific experience.**   Your background and experience need to tie in with the consultative solutions you provide. If you've never been in management, it will be difficult to advise on the topic

of management. If you've never been an entrepreneur, it will be hard to advise others on how to be a good entrepreneur. The exception to this, of course, is possessing a specialized knowledge that a manager or entrepreneur needs, such as operations, logistics, finance, and so on. The key is to make sure that the core solutions you offer as a consultant are those you have a lot of real-world experience in.

2. **Entrepreneurial experience.** Different from the first point, here I mean that as an independent consultant you will be an entrepreneur. If you've never done anything entrepreneurial before it will be more difficult for you to succeed. This isn't to say you can't succeed, but having actual entrepreneurial experience is a very nice benefit to have in this endeavor.

3. **Analytical experience.** While there is no magic recipe for the traits and characteristics that make for a successful consultant, being a good problem solver is a trait that would come close to the top if such a list existed. Regardless of the kinds of services you offer, almost all such work starts with figuring out what the problem is. Being analytical and good at solving complex problems will definitely help you succeed in this role.

4. **Sales and marketing experience.** While I can give you a ton of tips, methods, and tools to help you market and sell your services much more effectively, having professional sales and marketing experience will be a big plus for you. You will be the sales and marketing force for your company. Many consultants make a big mistake in assuming that sales is not something any university grants a degree in, thus it is easy knowledge they can pick up by reading some sales books. On the contrary, sales is a dedicated profession that requires a lot of skill and proficiency to master, so if you've never sold anything professionally in your life, this could be a sizeable barrier to your success.

There is an incredibly wide range of experiences, talents, and strengths in the consulting community. There is no ideal template. The items above will definitely help, but the real key is in identifying what you are great at and building a business where people pay you for that ability. That is the starting point on the way to your ultimate success.

2

Build a Foundation That Supports Heavy Profits

Opening Your Doors

When it comes time to actually start your business there are certain steps you must take. In this chapter I will talk about what I call the mundane must-haves. These are, while boring I admit, things that you just can't build a profitable business without. Profits occupy the second floor of your business. That means they are built on top of the first floor, which is your marketing and sales activity. That floor, though, is built on top of the foundation of your house, things like your office, your billing systems, your brand, website, pricing structures, and so on. Too many consultants ignore the foundation and then wonder why they're struggling.

All of the steps in this chapter are things you need to do right up front, before you even think about speaking to your first prospect.

What Should You Call the Business?

It all starts with a name. Not to argue with Shakespeare, but the name you choose, unlike that of a rose, will indeed determine if it smells sweet or not. The name of your company is one of the most important things you can decide on, as it is a big part of that all-so-vital first impression.

Naming any business can be a difficult task, but it doesn't have to be insanely complicated. Important shouldn't translate to impossible in this exercise. There are companies out there that will build such fear and hype, then charge thousands or literally tens of thousands of dollars to help you select a name. But it shouldn't cost you *any* money and it shouldn't keep you up at night.

Follow these seven simple guidelines when selecting the name of your new company, and relax.

1. **Brandstorm it.** The first thing you should do is get some blank paper (a lot, perhaps). Like brainstorming, start jotting down names that you like. Do not judge them, just write them down. Let them flow. I would recommend coming up with at least 30 to 40 in this stage. Next you will start paring down that list.

2. **Make sure it's available.** Start removing names from your list by seeing if they are available. You can do this in two ways.

   a. **Domain search.** You're going to want to have a name for your company that you can brand on your website. Go to www .godaddy.com, enter a name idea, and click search, and it will tell you if that domain name is available. If you chose Johnson Consulting but www.johnsonconsulting.com isn't available, try some other domains like www.jconsult.com or www.johnson consultingllc.com. Just make sure that any variant you try is available as a ".com" (not .org, .net, .TV, etc.). Also be sure not to make it so convoluted that only you know how to spell it (e.g., Greg.Johnson.consulting.LLC.com). If you can't find a simple variant available, nix that business name off your list.

   b. **Web search.** Type in the name you are considering and see if any websites come up in your search results. You would definitely not want to select a name that some other company is already using, regardless of their domain name.

3. **Keep it simple.** The name should be simple, so avoid naming your company after something only industry insiders would know or appreciate (unless they will be your only clientele). Resist the urge to name your business after the Greek god of productivity or war. Avoid names that combine two descriptive words (e.g., Qualicoach or Growthcom) as they are difficult for anyone to spell, and they just sound awkward.

4. **Make it representative.** I named my company Innermetrix to represent the fact that we provided metrics that measured inner strengths and talents. Granted, had I known what I know now, perhaps I would have chosen a name slightly easier to spell, but I've worked hard to establish the brand of Innermetrix and wouldn't change it for anything now. The best names stand for what you believe in, and have real meaning for what you do or whom you help.

5. **Make it catchy.** Avoid using clichés or hyperbole in naming your business. Peak, Apex, Pinnacle, and Summit are descriptive, imply great success and height, but they're also insanely worn out and over-used. On the other hand, don't go so far in the other direction that you end up with "Johnson Consulting." Part of effective branding involves separating yourself from the crowd and standing

out. If the name is boring or sounds like every other company, it will only make it that much harder to achieve differentiation. Yahoo! or Google selected great names as far as standing apart and being catchy, while not making them complicated.

6. **Make it corporate.** Many consultants opt to name their consulting firm after themselves. While probably the norm for legal PLLCs, calling your business "John Smith Consulting" implies you are the business—and only you. Follow the old adage of "playing big until you are" and shoot for a name that represents a legal entity, not a human being. I know—Macy's, Johnson & Johnson, Kellogg's, and many other very successful companies were named after their founders, but you aren't entering the business field a hundred years ago. Most of the large consulting firms used founder's names as well, but they all started as legal or accounting firms too.

7. **Don't restrict geography.** Sometimes new consultants tie their brand to a specific city or region (e.g., New York Management Inc. or Southeastern Consulting), but unless you plan to do business only in the same geographic area, I advise against regional naming. As an independent business consultant you will quickly find that you have no geographic borders, which is one of the great aspects of this industry.

** If you're someone who likes to stop and complete each section of a book like this, I've provided a complete checklist in Appendix D where you can keep track of work done, such as deciding on the name of your business, and many other activities to come.

What Business Structure Should You Choose?

For the purposes of this book I will speak to the United States business market. Every country has its own set of policies and regulations, so I advise you to seek the counsel of a licensed attorney in your own market to make sure you decide on the best business structure for your specific business.

There are really only four types of business structure most consultants choose from. Each has its own unique set of strengths and weaknesses.

1. **Sole Proprietors** (taxed as 1040, Schedule C) are unincorporated businesses. They are also called independent contractors, consultants, or freelancers. There are no forms you need to fill out to start this type of business. The only thing you need to do is report your business income and expenses on your Form 1040 Schedule C. This is the easiest form of business to set up, and the easiest to dissolve, but it provides the least protection.

2. **C Corporations** (taxed as 1120) are incorporated businesses. Every form of business besides the sole proprietor is considered a separate entity, and this often provides a measure of legal and financial protection for the shareholders. The shareholders of corporations have limited liability protection, and corporations have full discretion over the amount of profits they can distribute or retain. Corporations are presumed to be for-profit entities, and as such they can have an unlimited number of years with losses (ask your accountant why that can be a good thing). Corporations must have at least one shareholder.

3. **S Corporations** (taxed as 1120S) have features similar to a partnership. An S Corporation must have at least one shareholder. If any shareholder provides services to the business, the S-Corp must pay that shareholder a reasonable salary. This salary is a separate payment from distributions of profits or losses. S Corporations have the same basic advantages and disadvantages of general or close corporations. When a standard corporation makes a profit, it pays a federal corporate income tax on the profit. If the company declares a dividend, the shareholders must report the dividend as personal income and pay more taxes. S Corporations avoid this double taxation (once at the corporate level and again at the personal level) because all income or loss is reported only once on the personal tax returns of the shareholders. However, like standard corporations (and unlike some partnerships), the S Corporation shareholders are exempt from personal liability for business debt.

4. **Limited Liability Partnerships or LLCs** (taxed as 1065) are unincorporated businesses. Like corporations, partnerships are separate entities from the shareholders. Unlike corporations, partnerships must have at lease one General Partner who assumes unlimited liability for the business. Partnerships must also have at least two shareholders. Partnerships distribute all profits and

losses to their shareholders without regard for any profits retained by the business for cash flow purposes. Many business professionals believe LLCs present a superior alternative to corporations and partnerships because LLCs combine many of the advantages of both. With an LLC, the owners can have the corporate liability protection for their personal assets from business debt as well as the tax advantages of partnerships or S Corporations.

There are also trusts and non-profit structures, but I'm not aware of any consultants who have ever chosen either of these. If you have any questions about which structure is right for you, it is best to consult with your attorney or accountant. Taxation and liability issues are the two strongest determining factors for deciding to seek their counsel.

Should You Have Insurance?

The topic of business insurance is an important one, and something I strongly recommend you consider carefully. While I will give you some insight here, I also strongly recommend that you speak with an insurance broker who can give you much better advice.

Many new consultants mistakenly skip what they consider to be an unnecessary expense in their fledgling business (where cash is king). I recommend you consider minimal business insurance, as inadequate levels of protection put all your hard work at risk.

Let's explore the different kinds of insurance you could consider, and explain why each would benefit you and when you might consider purchasing them.

There are basically **seven** different types of insurance:

1. **Property insurance.** This insures against loss or damage to your business equipment, or to the property of others when they are in your location of business. Many consultants assume, incorrectly, that their homeowner's insurance will cover all of their valuable materials and equipment in the event of damage or loss, but this is not always the case. Many personal homeowners policies have exemptions for items belonging to a legitimate business run out of the house. You are going to make a nice investment in computers, printers, and other business items, so I recommend speaking to your

insurance agent about what options you have very early in the life of your business.

2. **Liability insurance.** Given today's litigious society, I don't think I need to explain why liability insurance is a good thing. The general public's view is that if you own your own business, you must be rich. While far from true, someone who feels wronged by you (or sees an opportunity to claim they were wronged by you) likely sees you as rich. Liability insurance protects you against lawsuits for negligence. If a client decides to sue you for damages there doesn't have to be any merit behind that suit to actually bring it, and it can cost you more in defending a spurious suit than you can afford. Thankfully, I've never personally been involved in any legal suit whatsoever, but unlike some other types of insurance, I strongly recommend you secure a liability insurance policy very early on as well.

3. **Casualty insurance.** Property and casualty insurance are commonly bundled together, so investigate that with your insurance agent, but they cover slightly different things. While property insurance will cover the loss of tangible property (from fire, theft, floods, etc.), casualty speaks more to things like loss of business, business interruption, continuance of business, and so on. A fire at your home or office may destroy your computer, and it is covered under your property insurance. The files you had on that computer are also lost—meaning you can't deliver on your commitment to a client, or are unable to do business—and casualty insurance would cover that, not property insurance.

4. **Commercial auto.** If you incorporate your business and transfer ownership of your personal vehicle to that business, your personal auto policy will not cover loss or liability associated with that vehicle. I've seen a few cases where the insurance company claimed a consultant used his vehicle primarily for work rather than personal, and refused to cover losses associated with an accident. Best to be safe and give careful consideration to purchasing a separate commercial policy from your agent. Having an at-fault accident that seriously injures or kills someone, without proper insurance, could open up a channel to sue your company as well as yourself individually (another reason why business liability is so important).

5. **Healthcare insurance.** This is unlikely to be of concern in any early stage practice, but if and when you get to a point where you

hire employees, this would be a requirement. That said, there are attractive group policies that can provide you with discounted health insurance through your business, which will lower the costs of carrying a private health insurance policy.

6. **Life and disability insurance.** This would only be of interest if you share the company with more than one shareholder. Were you to be injured and unable to work in the business, or killed, such a policy would pay out to the remaining shareholders of the business to cover that loss of key personnel. I've seen some cases where the remaining shareholders use proceeds from such a policy to buy out the shares granted to the survivors of the deceased business partner (after receiving his or her shares in the will). It's something to consider, but not one that needs to be done early in most cases.

7. **Worker's compensation.** If and when you get to the point where you hire real employees (not contracted 1099 workers), you will be required to open a worker's compensation policy by most states in the United States. Other countries have similar requirements. Not something to waste any time on until you grow to that point, though.

I highly recommend you investigate and purchase the first two types of insurance right off the bat (Property and Liability) with Liability being the most important in my opinion. Casualty will likely be bundled with Property, so the third insurance listed above would be the next most immediate thing to consider. The rest are valuable, but only at certain stages of your business, so you can revisit them when the time is right.

The Importance of Planning

Too many new consultants fail to establish a sound business plan right up front. As important an aspect as having a sound business plan is, however, I will not be diving too deeply into this topic as we could easily get lost. I will, however, recommend an action that will allow you to save time, yet still allow you to create a very well-constructed plan. And that's the rub, managing to create a very solid business plan that actually delivers value, but not spend months doing it.

Also, a good plan is a process, not a static event. One of the biggest mistakes any business owner makes is to create a strategic business plan in the beginning of their company, then leave it in a drawer forgotten and useless. A good plan is dynamic, meaning it is built to be changed or modified as the business grows. Its structure is one that is flexible, and to me the most important part is that such flexibility is quick and painless, since if it sucks to change it, it usually doesn't get changed.

For years now I've personally benefited from being able to develop a very strong business plan for my own businesses, yet not having to invest countless hours to get it done. I've done that by using the "One-Page Business Plan," based on a book of the same name written by Jim Horan. Since the two most important parts of such a plan are content and speed, this has been my solution of choice.

If you're an expert in building business plans, and that's one of the things you will be providing to your consulting clients, then by all means listen to your own expertise. However, if this isn't something you're an expert in, I highly recommend you not spend hours researching, learning, and inventing your own wheel. Instead just invest $39 and purchase the One-Page Business Plan (Professional Consultant's Edition) from their website.

That website: www.onepagebusinessplan.com

Once you get a plan—wherever you get it—just be sure to use and follow it, as it is definitely something that will greatly add to your chances of success.

The Critical Importance of Branding

You can't underestimate the importance of branding. Assuming that a moderately good name, and some logo that was designed by their significant other, will suffice, many consultants fail to fully appreciate the role that proper branding plays in creating a profitable consulting practice. In my opinion, effective marketing is impossible without a strong brand.

A good brand strategy rolls multiple pieces of your strategy into a single cohesive plan. After naming your company, creating your brand image and strategy should be the next thing you do. You will integrate your brand into everything, from marketing materials to business cards to your social media and online presence—everything.

What exactly is a brand? Literally defined a brand is, "Name, term, design, symbol, or any other feature that identifies one seller's goods or services as distinct from those of others." Practically defined, a brand "represents the quality, uniqueness, professionalism and value of your company and what it offers."

A strong brand:

- Explains who you are to your market.
- Attracts the right clients.
- Differentiates you from your competition.
- Represents the value and quality of your business's mission.
- Conveys the trustworthiness and reliability you seek to deliver.
- Makes a promise of what clients can expect from your company.
- Highlights your professionalism.

There are five steps to take when creating your brand:

1. **Start with your rough draft mission statement.** What is it exactly that your company seeks to do for your clients? Mission statements are short on detail and intended to capture the essence of your company's purpose. Craft a rough draft of your mission statement right now; we'll come back to it in later chapters and refine it to make it permanent.

2. **Design the brand logo/image.** Get professional help. Once you can clearly state your company's mission, seek out a professional logo design firm. Trust me, using crayons, a kitchen table, and selecting stock logos from your computer's Graphic Art folder will not suffice at all. If you can't find someone local who you like or can afford, try www.99designs.com, where you can post your request for a logo design and numerous graphic artists will submit concepts. Fees are ridiculously affordable on this site. Research shows that people remember what they see better than what they read, so your visual brand image needs to be very strong and expressive. Keep it simple, not too flashy and not at all complicated. A good litmus test is to ask others to tell you what they think the image represents. If they have no clue, or it's way off the mark, change it.

3. **Protect your brand.** Once you have a logo you love, you need to protect it by trademarking it. Some skip this step, but why in the world would you not bother to protect the visual image that represents your entire company? You can either visit www.legalzoom.com

and use their "everything done for you" process (that's not the real name by the way), which runs approximately $169, or do it yourself directly through the US Patent and Trademark Office by going to www.ustpo.gov and clicking on "trademarks." Doing it yourself is not difficult, but as with everything, you should always consider that time is money. And once you get your trademark, be sure to show that protection in your actual image by adding the trademark symbol (^{TM}) as part of the actual image file.

4. **Give your brand a tag line.** Images can be powerful and should convey a message but using a tag line as part of that image helps ensure your clients understand it that much more. Write a brief but meaningful tag line that captures the essence of your value proposition to all who will see it. One of my brands reads, "Talent. Find it. Develop it. Keep it." This pretty much captures the mission statement for that division.

5. **Proliferate your brand.** Once you have your brand image (logo), use it everywhere, and I mean *everywhere*. The more places people see your brand, the more powerful it becomes. Place it on letterhead, business cards, website, e-mail signature, marketing brochures, PowerPoint presentations, videos, articles, social media (use it as your picture instead of your beautiful mug). *Everywhere!*

All of this is why you don't want to skimp when it comes to developing your brand message and imagery. Do this right, as changing your brand down the road, or sticking to a crappy brand, is very costly in all the wrong ways.

What Business Supplies/Materials Will You Need?

Some experts will tell you that you need to invest in a ton of expensive, high-end equipment and supplies to get started. While this certainly doesn't hurt, it definitely isn't necessary either.

One of the benefits of this career is the low cost of doing business. Your overhead in the beginning can be very low, and if you require more expensive supplies and materials, you can grow into those as your revenues grow, but you can definitely start generating revenue without them.

That said, there are some basics that you simply *must* have, and at a certain level in order to appear professional, competent, and worthy of your prospect's business. Let's break those down into three essentials.

Basic Equipment

The three basic pieces of equipment that you must have are:

1. **Computer.** You don't have to spend several thousand dollars on the latest and greatest Mac, but you will have to have a computer and it needs to be newer (i.e., no older than two years). Reason being, you will need to do lots of e-mailing, Internet searches, and marketing, and create a multitude of documents. Whether you go PC or Mac, it is strongly advisable to have Microsoft software capabilities, as most companies work in Word, Excel, and PowerPoint. I am a huge champion of Apple and everyone here at IMX uses Macs. However, they all have Microsoft software packages so that even from a Mac we can work with all the same Microsoft documents. Whatever you choose, make sure you have a solid computer that has plenty of processing power, is up to date, and can work with all the new program files out there. I would recommend buying a brand new one to ensure it is optimal, and if you go with Dell or other PC versions, you're only talking $500 to $1,000 total.

2. **Internet Service Provider (ISP).** It should go without saying, but make sure you have a high-bandwidth Internet connection. Most consultants get it from the local cable television or phone providers, but make sure you get one of the highest packages when it comes to upload and download speed. Limiting yourself here will negatively affect your ability to conduct webinars, send and receive files, or even conduct effective e-mail marketing campaigns.

3. **Printer/Scanner/Fax (or Copy).** The only other truly required piece of equipment that you need is some form of printer. If you do purchase a new computer, more often than not they either offer a free printer with it, or a significantly discounted one. If you're going to purchase a printer I strongly recommend it be one of the combination devices that merges a printer, a scanner, a fax machine, and copier all into one. You will need to print high-quality proposals or even brochures to hand to clients, so it shouldn't be a cheap printer. You will need to scan documents

into your computer as well. As for the fax, it's not terribly important so don't worry too much about that. As long as you have a scanner, you can use online faxing services like www.pamfax.com for almost nothing. You don't need some large office machine, just one of the normal desktop models that cost anywhere from $150 to $300 max. I wouldn't worry much about "speed of printing/copying pages" as this is one of the big features they tout to justify cost. You're not going to be printing 1,000 pages or copies of anything any time soon. Choose superior quality printing, not volume.

Business Cards, E-Mail, and Letterhead

Three supplementary business necessities are:

1. **Business cards.** Business cards are crucial and one of the easiest ways to connect with prospective clients and reinforce your brand. I recommend ordering them before you open shop, and hand them out prolifically once you do. There are a couple of general rules about business cards:

   a. **They shouldn't cost you a ton.** There are online printing companies (e.g., www.overnightprints.com, or www.vistaprint .com) where you can order 1,000 high-quality, full-color premium business cards for as little as $35 delivered! This is the service I still use. These aren't poor-quality cards either. You could opt to visit your local printer, but you'll pay twice as much as you would online.

   b. **Writable.** Some cards can come with glossy finishes. This is cool on the front, but give the back of the card a matte finish so it can be easily written on. Taking notes on the back of a card is a good way to remind whoever takes your card of some specific thing they are to send you or remember.

   c. **Do _not_ make your own.** I can't tell you how many times I've been handed a business card from a new consultant and it is blatantly obvious it was printed on their home printer. The edges are perforated, it's a flat coating, and the printing is blurred. If you want to make sure you never get business, just take this route and hand something like that to a prospect. It screams, "I'm no good at this because I have so few clients that I can't even afford $35 for good business cards."

d. **Content.** Don't go crazy on a business card. Trying to stuff everything you can onto a card only leads to small print no one can read, or a cluttered look that isn't appealing. Your cards don't have to be elaborate. On the sites I mentioned above you can find tons of templates. I keep mine simple with just the following:
  i. Name and title (front)
  ii. Brand or logo (front)
  iii. Contact info (back)
  iv. Value proposition or tag line of what you do in terms that anyone can understand (front)
2. **E-mail.** E-mail is absolutely vital as it will be your primary means of communication with most of your prospects. Therefore, it has to be a program you understand how to use and one that allows you to easily track or find e-mails.
   a. **E-mail address.** Whatever you do—and I mean, *whatever you do*—I beg you not to use an AOL, Yahoo!, or Hotmail e-mail domain! Much like the impression a homemade business card makes, having an e-mail with one of these domains screams amateur. In the later section, *Website*, learn more about how to get your own business domain. It's very simple and inexpensive to set up your own business domain and have an e-mail associated with it. On any domain registration site (e.g., www.godaddy.com) you can search for a website name that is available and purchase that domain address for as little as $12 a year, and that includes free e-mail!
   b. **Branding.** Your e-mail is a great means of branding yourself, so make sure you use a signature in your e-mail that automatically places your contact information and brand at the bottom of each e-mail. Include everything you have on your business card, including your logo, contact info, website, and marketing message. It's also ideal to include your social media links as well. Warning, though, try not to add everything including the kitchen sink in your signature or tag line. I get e-mails from some consultants that have—and I just counted one yesterday—12 accreditations after their name (certified this or that, CBS, PhD, CHMD&##@$!). It's obnoxious and ineffective. Also, there seems to be some trend lately where consultants are placing some lengthy disclaimer at the bottom of their e-mails that

appears to speak to confidentiality of the contents of this e-mail (if you're not the intended receiver, yada, yada). Some of these things are their own small paragraph long. My advice—don't, as it's basically annoying as hell, and seeking to impose a contractual obligation unilaterally has absolutely zero legal merit.

3. **Letterhead.** While much of your correspondence with clients will be electronic, you will definitely need some letterhead for when you send physical proposals or invoices out. You should consider two types of letterhead: digital and formal.

   a. **Digital letterhead** is simply a Word document saved on your desktop that is a blank page with your logo on top and contact or website in the footer. Some make it more aesthetically pleasing by adding a watermark or phrasing down the side. This is fine, just don't overdo it. Create this Word page and save it to your desktop where you can find it easily. If you need to submit something to a prospect or client, pull it up, add your text, save it under another name (Acme proposal) and you're good to go. Understand, though, that this is digital, meaning it is to be used digitally. Only use this letterhead when e-mailing a document. It is not to be printed.

   b. **Formal letterhead** looks exactly like your digital letterhead, but it has been printed by a professional printing company because this is what you will use whenever you need to physically send something to a client. Like business cards, you can choose to go to your local printer and spend a lot of money, or you can visit the exact same online print shops and receive absolutely beautiful paper. Overnightprints.com sells 1,000 pages for as little as $70, and they deliver in less than one week.

Consistent branding is key. Across all platforms (e-mail signature, letterhead, business cards, etc.) make sure you stick to the same message, same logo, and always reinforce the same branding.

Brochures/Marketing Collateral

Brochures are a very important part of your branding and marketing success, but not in the way you may think. They convey who you are, what you do, and present you as a professional. At the same time, though, many new consultants make the mistake of relying too heavily on their brochures and investing too much money in them.

Much like the digital letterhead I just discussed, most of the brochures I send out are digital. They are one-page PDF documents that I attach to an e-mail, or that can be downloaded from my website.

The old-school mentality was that in order to be professional you had to invest thousands in printing very high-end, full-color, two-sided glossy folders with pockets. Nowadays I rarely if ever use them. At best you might want to print a small amount that you use only for delivering final proposals, but don't put you in debt. You could get perfectly professional, full-color, pocketed brochures for as little as 500 for $150. Of course, if it's the norm in your target market, you should adhere to the customary procedures. Nearly 100 percent of the time I meet with a prospect, I leave them with my business card and end up e-mailing the appropriate brochure to them when I follow up later that day.

General Rule of Thumb for Brochure Marketing

There is one rule when using brochures that you must pay attention to: Brochures never sell anything! Overloading the prospect with a seam-busting pile of pretty brochures that you hope will educate and impress enough to make a sale never works. In reality, the vast majority of brochures go straight in the circular file.

And as for educating and selling, you never want a piece of paper doing the selling for you. In some industries where the marketer is selling a commodity, fancy flyers and brochures might land business, but their sole purpose in your industry is to validate and support what you've already told them—never to do your job.

Tips on creating strong brochures:

- **Write from your reader's perspective.** Don't write what you want the reader to know. Write what you believe the reader wants to know. Sounds like a semantics issue, but when you change your perspective you will understand why it is not. First focus on the problem the reader is suffering from, then cover how you can help solve that problem. This is putting your value in context. Writing about what you do makes you the center of the topic, which should never be the case. The potential customer should always be the subject of discussion.

- **Design.** As with many other areas, I recommend you hire a professional graphic artist to create the brochure for you. Save money by having them create a theme or template, with which you can easily change the content. It creates consistency and avoids having to pay for new designs for every brochure. The online print shops can save you even more money, as they have templates already created by professional artists.
- **Use plenty of headers and subheaders.** Bear in mind that somewhere north of 90 percent of your readers will only skim your brochure. Pretend the reader only gets to see the headlines and subheaders, and make sure you get their attention. Break content up. A good brochure isn't a page full of text; instead, use short, digestible, power-packed groupings of words separated by lots of space.
- **Covers must grab attention.** Make sure your cover is designed to grab their attention—not pitch them. Beautiful things grab attention. The best approach I've found is to state the problem right on the cover (e.g., beautiful visuals, your logo, and the words, "Poor Leaders Killing Your Profits?").
- **Keep it simple.** Remember, brochures aren't meant to sell. They remind a prospect who you are, entice them to learn more, and add credibility to your business. Don't fill every inch with words or clutter. Don't try to sell the readers, just inform them. Blank space is very good. Don't use fancy words or technical jargon. Write to the average eighth grade reading level. Keep it concise.
- **Social proof rocks.** Social proof (testimonials, quantifiable stats) means more to the reader than anything you could ever say. Try to include quotes from existing clients in very brief sentences.
- **Provide a real call to action.** A common mistake is not providing a solid call to action. Consultants will place their contact information with just some weak suggestion ("To learn more, contact us here") and wonder why no one ever calls. While it's very important to always include all forms of contact, it's just as important to give a cogent call to action ("For a free copy of the research or article, visit our website.").

Phone Lines

The phone service you choose can completely make or break your business, and that's not hyperbole. Unfortunately, I'm constantly running into consultants who have some less-than-optimal phone service and I struggle to reach them or hear them, if we do actually connect. Here are **five** general principles for choosing your phone service:

1. **Separation.** Separate your business line from all other phone lines you have. Don't use an existing line at your house. Today, most phones show caller ID, and when you call from home it may show your last name, or worse yet, your spouse's name if he or she was the one to set up the account.

2. **Fidelity.** Currently lots of small or home-based business services are moving to some Voice Over Internet Protocol (VOIP) system as their primary office line. Perhaps in the future these services will work better, but I haven't found them to reach the level of reliability and sound quality they should have for professional services. I'm not saying you need to invest thousands in a professional phone system when you're working out of your den, but I wouldn't recommend you fall prey to the alluring low-price traps. I've just had too many calls with consultants using such services and struggled to hear anything they were saying, experienced drop calls, or ended up calling them on some other number. Play it cheap here, and suffer the consequences, I'm afraid. Go with a real landline.

3. **Voicemail versus answering machines.** Just as you separate your home phone from your business phone, I implore you to not use an old-fashioned answering machine either! All phone services now have voicemail functionality either included at no charge or for very little extra each month. Your prospect knows when you're running a physical answering machine, and nothing says, "Sorry I can't take your call right now but me and Uncle Rufus are getting Bessie unstuck out in the field" like the distinct beep of analog answering machines. I wish I didn't have to include some things like this in this book but, as amazing at it may be to you, I still get answering machines when I call some businesses. You need to be accessible to your prospects and clients, and in today's faster and furiously paced world of business, you need to be able to access messages from clients instantly.

4. **Conference lines.** One thing you will need is the ability to host a conference call with your clients. Many times there will be two or

more clients on the other end of the line, and nothing is worse than having to ask, "Could we use your conference line"? The great news is that there are all kinds of services where you can get a free conference line—absolutely free! Investigate them carefully as some market themselves when the person calls in. Check out the following examples and figure out which is best for you:

   a. www.gotowebinar.com
   b. www.freeconferencecalling.com
   c. www.freeconference.com

5. **Voice services.** You may want to consider going beyond simple voicemail and actually signing up for a slightly higher-end service.

   a. **Monitored answering services.** There are many different services now on the market that allow you to have an actual human answer your calls when you're not in. These are basically virtual phone attendants. These services can run as little as $35 per month, with no contract. The big benefit of this type of service would be to give the impression that you are bigger than you are, and they ensure that your customers feel well taken care of. If you're trying to keep expenses down, however, this should be considered carefully. There is a wide range of pricing so choose carefully and do your research.

   b. **Automated answering services.** A less expensive approach is to use an automated answering system where you set up multiple lines, each with its own mailbox, and the customer is routed to that line where they leave a message. In most cases these services work much like regular voicemail and notify you immediately of the voicemail, e-mail it to you where you can hear it, and even transcribe the voice message into text on your phone. This provides more options for your clients and makes a more professional image.

Stock Headshot

You will also need to have a high quality photo of yourself, or a "head shot." You will need it for press releases, your website, brochures, and other branding efforts, so make it a good one.

This isn't rocket science, but here are a few simple tips you should follow:

1. **Use a professional.** Many consultants mistakenly think that their personal camera will suffice and they have their friend snap a casual photo of them in their living room. Even though the average smartphone now takes High Definition photos, they aren't anywhere near the quality you need. The biggest factor in hiring a professional is their expertise in lighting and camera settings. You don't need to spend very much, but since you're won't likely need to repeat this step for quite some time, why not splurge.

2. **Just be you.** Whatever you do, don't go to the mall and get the cool packet where you are edited to death, positioned in front of some fancy backdrop, and have them add all kinds of cool effects (such as halo lighting behind your head). Keep it simple, professional, and straightforward. And no goofy poses either. Keep your hand off your chin— the Thinking Man has already been used. No looking over your shoulder unless you're wearing a wedding dress. Just a high quality, straightforward, neutral background with natural lighting only.

3. **Be professional.** This isn't your Facebook photo, so don't have your professional photo be of you in a T-shirt, climbing some mountain, or competing in the last Ironman race. Feel free to make it business casual if you want, but as the old saying goes, better to be overdressed than the other way around. Keep your target audience in mind. Dress how you would dress when making a call to their office. Also, solid colors are best as prints kill the eyes in photos.

4. **Smile, make eye contact.** Resist the urge to stare boldly into the camera, or make some fake expression. This is the Goldilocks of headshots, so don't be so serious that you look boring as hell, but don't take one with you looking like you just busted a gut at your old frat buddies' crude jokes either.

5. **Background.** As I said, stick to neutral backdrops that the photographer will have in his or her studio. Social media are fine for pictures of you walking on the beach or playing with the kids, but not here. And while I've seen some who promote a niche message (e.g., the Naval aviator who sells "Top Gun Leadership," or the accomplished adventurer who sells "Climbing the Leadership

Mountain"), I still recommend taking the professional consultant route and leaving the flight suit and climbing gear for the presentation slides or workshop flyers.

Webinar Capability

In today's wired world, one of your most effective marketing techniques will revolve around giving online educational lectures. When you're just speaking, a teleconference line works just fine. If you plan on sharing visual information with clients, you will need webinar capability. Webinars are simply online conferences where multiple people can join in and watch a presentation as well as interact.

Part of what I will teach you in the sales and marketing stages of this book will include using educational webinars as a marketing tool. It's an incredible way to market yourself, educate your prospects, and position yourself optimally for greater profits.

At this point in the process you only need concern yourself with acquiring the ability to conduct webinars. Most services are super simple to use and offer automated scheduling where your prospects can register on your website by using a single link. Most services even allow you to record the webinar as a video, to store on your website for anyone else to view in the future.

None of these services are truly free. That said, having webinar capabilities is vital. I recommend you find a provider and sign up for an account. While you will need to spend money, be wary of the plethora of high-priced alternatives out there. It's become a sales hotbed filled with people charging stupid-high fees when you just don't need them. Oh, and multilevel marketing companies have recently found this market, so be on the lookout for friends who come knocking on your door with the next big breakthrough in "video-conference." You don't need to pay the 20 people above him in the chain to get access to solid webinar services.

Establishing Your Internet Presence

In today's connected world if you don't have a web presence, you're dead . . . period! There may be those who argue otherwise, but then they are wrong. I personally remember the day when I could generate nice profits without a website, and definitely not a blog or any social media (which didn't even exist then). Of course I also remember the day I got my first pager and how business was conducted (or the lack thereof) before such technology arrived on the scene.

Distant memories aside, if you're going to build a profitable consulting practice today, you need a really good web presence. Why? Because in effect what a solid web presence does is level the playing field. Small businesses of the past were at a distinct disadvantage because promoting a brand cost a lot of money. There were printing costs, distribution, advertising space, and a host of other things that meant you needed to spend a hell of a lot of money to establish a well-known brand. Today, with a proper website, almost anyone can establish a well-known brand for literally pennies on the dollar.

It is this ability to effectively brand yourself, be visible to large audiences, and position yourself as the thought leader that have helped drive the popularity of independent management consulting.

Here's a good litmus test. Get online right now and search your name, or your company name. What did you find? How many pages did Google or Bing return? See my point?

A big mistake too many consultants make is that they have what I call "brochure sites" instead of lead-capture websites. Brochure sites are the old-fashioned kind of website that is basically like a brochure for your business, only online. It is great at explaining what you do, showing off your services, and providing contact information, but it is also static, one-dimensional, and most important it doesn't really do anything to generate leads. It may add credibility, but only for someone you've already met and told about the site. A lead-capture site, on the other hand, actually helps find those people to meet.

I will teach you how to actually use a lead-capture website when we get to the marketing chapters, but for now we're discussing set-up during this build phase, so here's what you should do.

To accomplish everything, you can choose to either do it yourself or hire the right professional. I'm so biased towards focusing your time on generating revenue that I am going to make the bold statement right here and say that, "If you insist on building your own website I'm not going to help"! Sure, you can secure a domain name, select a hosting plan, and pick your website, but trust me, unless you're very knowl-edgeable about all of these areas you will end up with just another brochure site. I've seen far too many consultants do it themselves and develop horrible websites that hurt their business more than help.

Ninty eight percent of consultants polled state that "getting more business" is their number one concern. Guess what? Approximately 95 percent of all consultants have brochure websites. Coincidence? Not that I'm saying a consultant's website is the only factor in profitability, but having the mentality of "I will save a few bucks and do it myself" is indeed a big part of the problem. Cheap business cards, e-mail, phone, brochures, and a website cobbled together as inexpensively as possible all contribute to those 98 percent who need more business.

Listen up, folks. Hire a professional to set your website up! And when you do, share the list of requirements below with him or her. Don't be the hobbyist here. You're attempting to create a legacy practice and you don't have time for experimenting and playing around. There's money to be made.

The first (and only) step: Print Figure 2.1 and hand it to the professional you hire to build your web presence.

A quick search of the Internet should return a ton of potential web developers to hire. Make sure the one you hire has experience in creating more dynamic websites that involve at least a blog, WordPress, and preferably Infusionsoft as well.

If you're having trouble finding the right person, I've used the same company for many years now. Every personal and corporate site I own was done through Jim Caudell over at TribeCoach.com. Not only are they awesome designers and exceptionally well priced, but their original backgrounds are in marketing so they get what I'm trying to do. And, the largest percentages of their clientele are independent consultants just like you and me. Check them out (www.tribecoach.com).

The only aspects of a brochure site your new website should retain are the basic informative parts. Do make sure your website has the following sections:

- **An introductory or landing page.** The landing page is the first thing your prospects will see so remember the first impression rule. Keep it professional, clean, and containing your Unique Value Proposition (which you will write in Chapter 5).

Dear Website Development Expert,

This fine consultant is going to need a website, blog, and social media outlets set up. This website will support their business by allowing them to:

- Make regular blog posts, so please consider using WordPress in the website.
- Capture leads (squeeze page style) on the site, so please consider Infusionsoft, AWeber or some similar auto-responder and double opt-in technology as well.
- Posting YouTube videos and podcasts.
- Social media accounts for: LinkedIn, Facebook (with fan page), Twitter, and YouTube.
- And please please please make sure the URL is a ".com" ONLY.

Thank you so much for your assistance.

Figure 2.1 Instructions to Web Developer

- **An "about us" page.** Provide a list of everyone who works in the firm, use your headshot if you want, but write a bio and end it by connecting to your Unique Value Proposition.
- **A "What we do" page.** This can be called a "services" page, or anything else you like, but the content of this page describes what services you provide. Another great place to drop your Unique Value Proposition.
- **Testimonials.** Always a good idea to have multiple testimonials or endorsements from folks. Make them one or two sentences maximum and pepper them around your site in different places and pages.
- **Your blog page.** This is a separate page that links to your blog.
- **A "Case Studies" page.** Once you have some experience and wins under your belt, it's great to add a "Case Study" page to your site where you can write up a short description of the problem a company was having, what you did to help them, and be sure to provide tangible results like savings or real numbers.
- **Contact page.** Be sure to have a stand-alone page where prospective clients can reach out to you in as many ways possible, and as easily as possible. Include every way you can think of to allow your prospect or client to reach you.

Since you're one smart cookie and you've taken my advice and plan on letting a professional design your website, there is one last piece you will want to do before handing the project over to that professional.

The most effective way to reach new prospects on the Internet is to have your website easily found on the Internet. This means you need to do some "keyword" research up front.

Whenever you search on the Internet for anything, you enter keywords and the engine returns the results and ranks them by relevance to those keywords. It is these keywords that play a huge role in your online marketing success. Almost no one ever goes past the first or second page of results.

Understanding the keywords you need to hand to your web developer is something only you can do. The good news is that the largest search engine company in the world gives you a free resource to make this step much easier.

Fire up your computer and head to the Google Keyword Search Tool.

Go here: https://adwords.google.com/o/KeywordTool.

Once you're there you can quickly learn how to enter keywords you think your prospects will use when trying to find a company like yours, the services they need or the problems they have.

What you get are some very cool things:

- The keyword you entered and how many times it was searched for on the Internet.
- Recommendations for other keywords people also searched for.
- How competitive that keyword is, or how many other sites are using it as well.

I say this is cool because even if you're not sure which keywords to use, Google points you in the right direction. Grab a pen, try a bunch of keywords, and see which ones come back with the most searches. Ask your web designer about which words they think are best because things like the Long Tail effect, and other variables, can affect which ones will be the best. Once you get this list of keywords, keep them close because you will use them again later in this book.

Listing with Website Directories

You will want to ask your website developer to list your site with some website directories as well. This makes a big difference in ensuring your site is found when your prospects start searching for you.

Your website developer will have his or her own list of favorites, but here are ones I recommend as well. Some directories are free, others will cost you some money, but when it comes to websites, such investments are worth it, in my opinion.

- The DMOZ directory (www.dmoz.org)
- The Yahoo! directory (dir.yahoo.com)
- The Best of the Web directory (www.botw.org)
- The GoGuides.org directory (www.goguides.org)
- The Business.com directory (www.business.com/directory/)
- The What You Seek directory (www.whatuseek.com)
- The Joe Ant directory (www.joeant.com)

The last part of establishing your web presence is to set up your social media outlets. Websites have changed. We're not talking about the same web you may be familiar with. The old World Wide Web was mostly a static world where users were left to experience a website in one direction. They could read and take from the website, but not contribute or interact beyond the minimal list of ways. It was a passive experience for the most part.

Welcome to Web 2.0, the term coined to reflect modern websites that use truly interactive technology to create user-generated content, true discussions, and living dynamic experiences online. On Web 2.0 websites the user is not only a part of the experience, but helps build that experience. This is important because as a consultant your success requires you to build relationships.

A good Web 2.0 presence consists of the following:

- A lead-capture website
- A blog
- Video and podcast posts
- The following social media accounts:
  - LinkedIn (www.linkedin.com)
  - Facebook (www.facebook.com)
  - Twitter (www.twitter.com)
  - YouTube (www.youtube.com)

As for these social media sites, they are super-simple to set up. Using them effectively for marketing is a bit of a different story, but I will cover that specifically in Chapter 6. For now, let's just focus on getting them set up.

You don't need a separate set of instructions for each of these, as they are all very user-friendly. Your task right now should be to put this book down, get online, and visit each of the four sites above and create an account. Be sure to complete the profiles because a more complete profile will help you create a large and lucrative network. You don't have to post anything just yet, just get the account opened.

Once you have these created, the only other thing to do at this stage is to let your website developer know so he or she can link them to your website.

Banking

It should go without stating that you will need a professional bank account. Similar to the e-mail and phone discussions, don't be the hobbyist who doesn't bother to set up a formal corporate bank account. Legally, it can make it a nightmare to do your taxes, and it can be questionably legal to commingle funds anyway.

One of the most important things you will need with your bank account is a "merchant services account." This means you have the ability to accept credit card payments. Some clients may want to pay in this way. Many executive coaching relationships require payment for the upcoming month in advance, and it's typical to keep the client's credit card information on file and charge it automatically each month. If you plan to sell seats at workshops or webinars, you will need this capability as well. Even if the customer pays you with a check, depositing it into the account of "John and Mary Smith" looks really bad.

Some consultants balk at paying the minuscule rates that credit cards charge, but the 2 to 3 percent they charge is well worth the ease and impression. Some refuse to use American Express because it charges 4 percent, but think how small you appear when you say, "Sorry, but we don't accept American Express." You just joined the ranks of the mom-n-pop diner down the street.

Choose a bank you're comfortable with, and talk with them about what they offer in the way of a high-quality merchant account.

Do You Need an Office?

There was a time where not having a physical office space really hindered how successful you could be and what impression you made on your clients. This isn't the case anymore, especially in this career. With the advent of technology you can provide nearly identical service to your clients from the comfort of your own home.

The majority of consultants I know started out of their house. Remember, in your practice's infancy conserving cash is one of your top priorities. The added expense of a physical office lease can be sizeable and damaging. If there was great justification for it, I would back your doing so, but there's just not. With all the technology and virtual services I've already mentioned, there is almost nothing you can't do from home. My own practice was able to grow just fine with me working completely from home for many years. It was only once we started conducting lots of regular in-house training that we had to move into the nearly 8,000 square feet we now occupy. If I could still avoid the overhead I sure would, so don't be in any rush.

One thing to consider is that almost all of your business meetings will take place at your prospect or client's office. I don't remember the last time a client came to me (outside of training). It just doesn't happen.

If you are working from home, though, I'm still a big believer in establishing a regular schedule, carving out a secure space in your home that is for work only, protected from outside noise, and has a dedicated phone line. You make a horrible impression when your prospect hears dogs barking, children crying, or doorbells in the background. If I'm your client it is actually somewhat insulting to have to be interrupted like this.

The downside to working from home is that it can make it that much easier to run your business like a hobby. While it's wonderful to walk down the stairs, grab some coffee, kiss your spouse, and walk 25 feet to work each morning, I caution that it can lead to a level of informality that undermines success. For this reason I think a true office is better in some ways, but *only* when you can afford it.

Reason being, it helps ensure you are building a legacy business, not a hobby. Having a real office helps separate work from home. It reduces distractions in most cases, and I find there is some subtle change in mindset when you're working from a professional location where "business" happens, not personal life.

Moving to a physical office doesn't mean you have to go broke either. Many consultants are now taking advantage of one of the most incredible opportunities I think they could have—virtual office space. The concept has been around for years, but for you, the independent consultant, I think it is one of your greatest advantages.

There are tons of "virtual offices" around the world where you can rent micro space in a large office building along with other entrepreneurs. These spaces cater specifically to your needs by offering full-time, part-time, or as needed "furnished" office space. The big benefit is that they include common space you can share and schedule as needed. They have small and large board or meeting rooms. They staff full-time receptionists who can answer your business line (thus eliminating the need for virtual phone systems mentioned earlier). There are ancillary services like copying, faxing, even QuickBooks, and collection services, believe it or not. You receive a physical mailing address at a prestigious building in most cases, and if you need to meet with someone at your place they would experience entering a large building, being greeted by a receptionist, sitting in a well-appointed waiting area, and meeting you in a formal board room with Wi-Fi, digital projector, and even an IT support person who could help you figure out why your presentation isn't working.

If and when you get ready to move to a physical office space, this kind of virtual space would be the next step I'd advise. To learn what's available in your area, do an Internet search for "virtual office space" and see just how much they offer for so little cost. A good example of what you should be looking for would be Regus (www.regus.com) as one of the largest players in this space.

Software Programs

There are certain software programs that will help save you time as well, so you can spend even more time selling and generating revenue. Remember, as a small business it's vital that you find a way to decrease the amount of time you spend working "in" the business, and spend as much time as possible working "on" the business.

To help with that, here are a few programs you should consider using:

- **QuickBooks** (www.quickbooks.com). Unless you're outsourcing your bookkeeping to an accountant, QuickBooks is a great way to minimize the complexity and time you spend "in" your business. QuickBooks is a full accounting system that allows you to track expenses, create invoices, and organize all your financial data so that at the end of the year you simply send a file to your tax preparer and you're done.
- **FreshBooks** (www.freshbooks.com). This software program allows you to easily track time spent on any given project. While I will teach you later on why you should never charge your clients by the hour, being able to track time is very useful to understand whether you're actually charging adequately. Sometimes you think you can

do the work in X hours and charge accordingly, but having a simplified way of testing that through experience helps correct mistakes in future proposals.

- **TimeDriver** (www.timetrade.com). If you've ever spent time chasing 20 e-mails back and forth attempting to find a time that works for both you and your client, this software is perfect. You'd be amazed how much time gets sucked up in exchanging e-mails attempting to nail a time that works for meetings, or webinars, or coaching sessions. This software allows you to create openings in your calendar that your clients can see for themselves, pick one, and book (all without ever bothering you). This is wonderful for regular coaching calls, or support calls with clients.

- **Severa** (www.severa.com). You will definitely want to use some form of project management software, as tracking and reporting progress on projects is a vital part of delivering superior solutions and service. Old school consultants would track such things in a notepad, or homemade Excel doc. Such an approach is disorganized, easily lost, and worst of all takes too much time away from revenue generating work.

- **CRM Software.** You will benefit greatly from using some form of Customer Relations Management software (CRM). My two favorites are from Salesforce.com and ACT (www.act.com). Both handle the customer management side very well, but Salesforce.com tends to specialize in the sales tracking aspect a little more. Both are widely used, and a simple Google search of CRM or sales tracking software will return dozens more. As your database grows, such software will really help keep your network organized.

What Will Your Role Be?

An unfortunate mistake made far too often is to not stop and actually think through what your role will be. Taking an ad hoc, "I will do everything as it comes up" approach will surely lead to failure. Consider carefully what your natural talents, inclinations, strengths, and abilities are and how you can craft your role in a way that maximizes your strengths and minimizes your weaknesses as much as possible.

The Myth of Strengths and Weaknesses

Why is it so important to outsource those things you are not great at, or enjoy doing well? Wouldn't conventional wisdom argue that people should apply themselves and develop a strength where one doesn't exist? Shouldn't you fix those weaknesses? The answer is *no*, you definitely should not make your business dependent on your weaknesses or non-talents! The strengths and weaknesses I'm talking about aren't deficits in knowledge or experience. I'm speaking strictly to innate talents or traits that you cannot develop in a training program or by reading a book.

There is a myth about these natural strengths and weaknesses, one that states we all naturally possess them. In reality, we don't. What we do possess are natural talents and nontalents, but these are not the same as strengths and weaknesses. In reality, you only have *potential* strengths and *potential* weaknesses.

I'm simply not the type of person who thinks it's okay to disguise a weakness as an opportunity for development. I actually hate this term because more often than not it supports the incorrect view that I can fix a weakness by developing it into a strength. If one of my clients is suffering from a weakness I tell them so; but, the key is that this weakness isn't natural, it's manufactured. When you allow your success to depend on your talents, you create strengths. When you allow your success to depend on your nontalents, you create weaknesses.

Think of talents and nontalents like two boxes. The first box contains a gift (talent) and comes all gift wrapped with a bow. The second box contains trouble (nontalent) and is marked Pandora's box. Regardless of the contents, however, each box only contains potential. The first box is only potentially good, the latter only potentially bad. Nothing happens until you actually open the boxes.

If you never open the gift box, you never receive the gift contained inside. Likewise, if you never open Pandora's box, you never suffer the consequences. Talents and nontalents work in very much the same way. If you never rely on your talents (open the gift box) than you never realize the strengths contained inside. Likewise, if you never rely on your nontalents (open Pandora's box) then you never suffer the weaknesses contained inside.

What controls this potential is how you apply yourself. If you have a nontalent for strategic thinking and create dependence on that nontalent by selling strategic planning consulting to your clients, you just manufactured a weakness. If you make sure your success doesn't depend on you being a great strategic planner, however, then you don't manufacture a weakness for yourself. That nontalent remains only a potential weakness.

When you make this shift in perspectives and realize that any weaknesses you have only exist because you manufactured them, you should also realize that you could correct it by removing that dependence. And that's the exciting part. Just like Mom used to say, "I brought you into this world and I can take you out," so too did you bring your weaknesses into this world and so too can you take them out.

The most successful consultants understand this. They know that they are the only ones responsible for whether they benefit from strengths or suffer from weaknesses. They don't spend their time trying to fix their weaknesses. Instead they just make sure their success doesn't depend on their nontalents.

To make sure you don't manufacture any weaknesses, be sure to create a role for yourself that relies as much as possible on your natural strengths and as little as possible on your weaknesses. Give specific thought to what services you will provide and ask yourself if you're manufacturing a weakness by doing so. Take a look at the duties you have inside your own business. Are there tasks or responsibilities for which you have a weakness, yet you're the one who must do them? Could they be outsourced?

When Peter Drucker, the elder statesman of management wisdom, spoke to leaders about increasing performance in their people, he said, "Your job is to make the strengths of your people more effective and their weaknesses irrelevant." He didn't talk about correcting their weaknesses by developing new natural talents; he championed making them irrelevant (by not depending on them).

To help you with learning your greatest natural strengths and weaknesses, here's a link to complete one of my own online strengths profiles, which will help you discover or confirm your strengths and weaknesses. It takes roughly 10 minutes online and the results will come straight back to you, and only you, instantly. I highly recommend it! Once you get your results back, move on to the next exercise I provide below.

Go here to complete the Personal Strengths profile, and click on the "Profitable Consultant Strengths" link (www.theprofitableconsultant .com).

The CEO Bucket List

To further avoid manufacturing weaknesses in your business, here is a simple exercise to keep from going down the do-everything path. I call it "The CEO Bucket List," I like to say, "It's not what you want to do before you die. It's what you need to do before you kill yourself."

- **Step #1:** Complete the Personal Strengths profile (i.e., the DISC Index) through the link above. Become familiar with the specific strengths and weaknesses the report shows you and write down 5 to 10 of each.
- **Step #2:** Do what I call "task storming," which is where you grab some paper and start writing down every single task you do in any given day, week, or even month. Just as in brainstorming, don't qualify your tasks as you write them. Nothing is too mundane here. If you do it, then write it down. No columns, categories, anything. Just write one long list of everything you do in your role.
- **Step #3:** Now, based on your talents (i.e., strengths and weaknesses) and title (i.e., CEO), imagine you are sitting in front of three big buckets. The bucket immediately to your front is filled with all of those tasks you wrote down in step #2. The bucket to your left says "Me" on it and the bucket to your right says, "Not me." Both the "me" and "not me" buckets are empty. Your task is to imagine yourself pulling one single task at a time out of that bucket in front of you, examining it, and determining which of the other two buckets it should go in—again based on your talents and title. If a task is not something you have any talent for, throw it in the "not me" bucket. If the task is something you're pretty good at, but isn't something the CEO of the company should be doing, throw it in the "not me" bucket. For example, how much sense does it make to be doing your own admin work when your hourly rate is $150 to $300 an hour, and a virtual assistant could do it for $20 an hour? Conversely, if the task is something for which you have a natural affinity or talent, *and* something a CEO should be responsible for, throw it in the "me" bucket. In reality, as you walk through your paper list, mark each task as either "M" (for Me), or "NM" (for Not Me). Use whatever you want (e.g., +/−, yes/no, etc.) but make sure to mark every item on the original task-storming list as one or the other.

Are there things in your main bucket that you should put in the Not Me bucket, but simply can't afford to, or aren't comfortable doing yet? Absolutely. Perhaps you literally cannot afford to outsource some of these things, but the most important part is that you are even asking these kinds of questions. The number one danger of being an entrepreneur is falling into the do-everything trap. Since everyone has some number of things they suck at, when you do everything, you can rest assured that you will be manufacturing weaknesses.

Letting go can be scary. However, not delegating those things that don't fit your role, or don't maximize your greatest talents, will sap revenues big time. It's easy to follow the old "If you want something done right do it yourself" mantra. Trust me, don't do it! Do everything you can to avoid creating a role for yourself that manufactures a bunch of weaknesses.

The moral of the story here is, "Don't allow your success to depend on you being great at things you suck at!"

Outsourcing

Once you have completed the CEO Bucket List exercise, you will have a list of tasks or duties that you know you should avoid doing if at all possible. Realizing that you won't be able to get rid of all them, try asking, "Who can I get to do these things?" As the entrepreneur you enjoy the easiest role in existence when it comes to avoiding this dilemma. As the one responsible for crafting your own role, you don't need to convince anyone else what your duties should and shouldn't be. You're the boss so if you decide to do it, then problem solved.

But where to go to offload these tasks that still need to be done, but just not by you? The best way to do this is to outsource them.

I realize that it can cost money to outsource and the last thing you want to do in any new business is take cash away from the business, but trust me when I say that as soon as you can possibly do it . . . do it! The returns you will appreciate, and the time you can reinvest in applying your strengths and generating revenue, will be well worth it.

Common tasks I normally see consultants outsource include things like:

- Website development and management
- Scheduling/administrative work

- Graphic design
- Newsletter writing
- Bookkeeping
- Proposal writing
- Accounting and taxes
- Data entry
- Research

When you outsource, make sure the very first things you seek to hand off are non-revenue-generating tasks or duties. Such "time sucks" should be on the very top of your list. Nothing should be more understandable than the logic of "The more time you spend on things that don't directly generate revenue, the less revenue you will make."

As for where to outsource, you have two options. The first is to pay someone else to do it, and the second is to barter with someone else, which I'll cover next. There are all kinds of great resources out there for virtual assistants who can do a lot of the things in your "not me" bucket. I like to say that your task is to "Find someone who loves to do what you loathe to do." To learn more, here are a few sites I recommend, all of which screen any virtual assistant candidate quite rigorously.

- www.assistantmatch.com
- www.vanetworking.com
- www.resourcenation.com (search "virtual assistant")
- www.hiremymom.com (one of my personal favorites)

Poke around, learn what is out there, and give serious thought to outsourcing even just the worst offenders in your list. You'll be glad you did.

Talent Bartering

As for those things in your "not me" bucket that you can't afford financially to outsource, consider bringing back to life something that all cultures have done for millennia—bartering.

Talent bartering is when you partner with someone else to swap or barter each other's complementary talents.

Perhaps you need some website development work, so find a web designer who could use some business advice and offer to barter business consulting for website work. Maybe you need some light bookkeeping, so find a work-from-home bookkeeper that could use your coaching, and barter services. Independent lawyers could use help with coaching, strategic planning, marketing, even hiring staff—all of which you could provide in return for their advice or help.

Simply put, if there is something you need to outsource, but can't afford to pay someone else to do at this time, see if you can find someone who can do that work for you and make a trade of your expertise for theirs.

Hey, it may not be pigs for corn, but I've seen it work extremely well.

3

Poor Pricing Equals Poor Profits

The Money Side

In consulting, perhaps one of the most recurrent reasons for poor profits is undercharging. It's unfortunate, because it has less to do with not understanding what should be charged and more to do with the consultant's lack of confidence, insecurity, or most commonly desperation.

Let me share the story of a friend of mine named John Butler. John was a seven-figure management consultant in Dublin, Ireland, and he had been a client of mine before he passed away. John attended a conference I was hosting in Germany some years back, and over beers one night we got to talking about this vexing issue, and how so many other consultants we knew suffered from it.

John had indeed built a very profitable practice years earlier, but he had grown tired of working so hard and was considering retiring from the 80-hour-a-week job he'd built for himself. He wanted to pull the throttle back and relax a bit.

He struggled with the thought of having to let clients go, so he figured the best way to avoid that confrontation was to get the clients to voluntarily leave him instead. He decided that if he raised his prices significantly, enough clients would walk away, and if he did keep some small percentage of his clients the addition in fees would cover the losses. Near the end of one year John informed all of his clients that he would be quadrupling his fees!

Thinking that this move would surely thin out his client base, imagine the shock when he found out he had only lost approximately 20 percent of his customers! And thus John's profits skyrocketed into the seven-figure range.

The moral here is that too many consultants think it's safer to charge less and get at least some business than charge more and risk not getting any. In reality you'd be surprised at how charging more doesn't scare off clients as much as you may think. I would argue that it actually only scares away the cheap ones you don't want anyway, and it creates the impression of superior value in all the ones you do want.

Scary as it may be, especially for a newcomer, do not undervalue your worth, do not set low prices, and do not settle for checking a win in the "Got a client" box, only to find you are unable to check the "Made enough money to pay the mortgage" box.

In the following steps, I will discuss the keys to setting your best price, sticking to it, and making sure your practice is highly profitable.

Determining Your True Hourly Base Rate

Time to start deciding what you will charge. The first thing you need to do is to determine your "true hourly base rate." However, this rate is for your information only, *not* for your clients. It is the hourly price you will use to calculate what you will charge based on the overall effort you will put in, and the return you would like to get for that effort. It is *not* the figure you will tell the client you charge per hour. Even though it won't be used on all types of pricing structures, it's an important number to understand regardless of the pricing model you use.

To calculate your total base hourly rate, you need to fill in the following variables:

A. Desired annual revenue $ _____
B. Number of work weeks (annually) _____
C. Number of hours worked per week _____
D. Working base rate (TBD) _____
E. True hourly base rate (TBD) _____

Once you have these figures you want to plug them into the following formula:

$$\frac{A}{(B \times C)} = (D \times 2) = E$$

In this formula you have:

- A (which is the total desired revenue annually) divided by:
- B × C (which is the sum of total weeks worked in a year multiplied by number of hours worked per week), which gives you:
- D—your working base rate (D).

■ The last step, since you will never work 100 percent of your week delivering services for fees (think sales and marketing time, administration, networking, hand holding, project updates, travel, etc.) is to assume that at best you get to spend 50 percent of your week delivering revenue-generating work. So, you multiply "D" (your working base rate) times two (2) to arrive at:

■ E—your true hourly base rate.

Here's a real-life example:

$$\underset{\text{Annual hours}}{\underset{\nearrow}{\frac{\overset{\overset{\text{Annual revenue}}{\searrow}}{\$100,000}}{(1,920\text{hrs})}}} = \underset{\searrow}{(\$5\overset{\overset{\text{Working base rate}}{\frown}}{2} \times 2)} = \$104 \text{ per hr}$$

True hourly base rate

■ You want to make $100,000 in a year (A).
■ You start with 52 weeks in a year, but subtract 4 for vacation, sick leave, holidays, and so on, so you have 48 weeks of work in that year (B).
■ You take an average of 40 hours worked per week (C).
■ You multiply 48 times 40 (work weeks × work hours per week) and get total hours worked in a year as 1,920 (B × C).
■ You divide annual revenue by total hours worked (100,000 divided by 1,920) to get your working base rate of $52 (D).
■ To adjust for true hours worked, you multiply that working base rate times two (2) to arrive at your final true hourly base rate of $104 per hour (E).

However, you're still not finished because you will have expenses. Even working from your house you will have Internet bills, cable, phone, supplies, non-reimbursed travel expenses, membership fees, and so on.

You need to add your operating expenses into your true hourly base rate to make sure you cover those costs as well. A good rule of thumb is to use 10 percent of your projected revenue for expenses or the cost of doing business. Obviously this figure can vary widely, but it will work well for now. Once you get your business running you can come back and revisit true expenses if need be.

The fastest way to do this is to simply take 10 percent of your true hourly base rate and add it on. In the example above, my true hourly base rate is $104.00. Ten percent of that is $10.40. Combine them and you arrive at $114.40, but keeping it easy, round it up to $115.00 per hour, and *that's* the figure you should use in some of the fee structures we will tackle next.

I've created an automated Excel spreadsheet that will help do these calculations for you. Visit www.innermetrix.com and look under the "Consultant Support Library" to download it.

Types of Fee Structures and Benefits

There are a wide variety of fee structures you can choose from. The most difficult thing when new to consulting is figuring out which one is right for you. Most consultants use several of these models depending on who they are working with and what they are delivering.

The reality is that the best way to learn which one is best for your practice is by trial and error. Unavoidably, you will test many of them and decide for yourself which ones you like and don't like, because much of the success of each of these depends heavily on you, your clients, and your offerings. I will, however, walk through each and give you the general principles and strengths and weaknesses of each, to help speed your learning curve.

There are two core categories of fee structures you could consider: task-based and value-based.

Task-Based Fee Structures

Task-based fees focus on the tasks that you do and how many total hours you work. They focus much less (if at all) on the overall value you deliver. For some specific engagements they may actually work, but there are sizeable downsides to this structure that must be understood, because while you may feel you're delivering value, in reality you are an expense—separated from the end objective's value. And nothing good ever comes from being seen as an *expense*.

The three traditional types of task-based structures are:

1. **Hourly Fees:** An hourly-based fee structure is simply that—you charge the client a flat hourly rate, you work the hours you need to complete the work, and they pay you. Simple, right? Granted, from a logistics standpoint it is the simplest of the fee structures. But you need to be sure to include all the hours you work. Don't forget travel time to and from the work site.

   The big problem with an hourly rate, and the main reason why I *rarely if ever* recommend it, is because it cheapens your value. As a consultant you need to be valued for improving the client's overall condition (sound familiar yet?). Hourly rates, though, compensate you for how many hours you work—regardless of outcome. Forget the high-priced attorneys you know. Consulting is *not* the same. An hourly program turns you into a subcontractor, not an authority. You become a commodity.

   It also limits results because if you find there is more work to be done once you're inside (something more common than you may think), you are left to either add the hours without permission and be seen as padding your bill, or find yourself asking the client to approve more hours and money. Creating yet another point where the client must decide whether to spend more money is never good. Winning a sale is hard, so why would you create the need to win yet more sales competitions? More importantly, you've made the cardinal sin of separating your true value from results.

   This transactional approach *may* work if the client only needs a transactional solution (speaking, joining them at a conference, sitting on a panel to interview potential hires, etc.) but always delivers the shortest-lived revenue and the lowest overall profits. I recommend you avoid it like the plague.

2. **Per Diem Fees:** Per diem (or "per day") fees are very similar to hourly-based fees. The difference is you charge a single fee for "a day," which is somewhat subjective. Is that a six-hour day? An eight-hour day? All these are things you need to consider before charging a per diem fee.

   Like hourly fees, this is one of the easier pricing models. Using your handy-dandy true hourly base rate you simply determine what a full day is and multiply that times your true hourly base rate. As I stated above, unless you're charging by the hour, never share your total hourly base rate with clients. It is a figure for you to use in determining rates like this. If there's significant expense involved (airfare, hotel, etc.) most consultants will charge "per diem plus expenses."

Like hourly fees, per diem fees risk disvaluing your true benefit to the client. They turn your relationship into a transactional one, wherein they bought your services for a day (or five) and you're now their hired gun. After your day is over, they're through with you. Your true value wasn't focused on the results as much as it was on the time you put in.

Outside of unique instances such as speaking, attending a conference, representing the client at some function, conducting stand-alone training, or some similar "one-off" interaction where your value is only intended to be short lived, I usually don't recommend a per diem fee structure either.

3. **Retainer Fees:** A retainer is somewhere betwixt and between in the task-based versus value-based argument. In some ways it is part task-based, as you are being paid a flat fee for providing a set number of hours of work or availability. Yet, in other ways a retainer is a value-based arrangement if you build it so it covers your being on-call for advice, counsel, hand-holding, light work and the like. Either way, retainers make great sense, and I strongly recommend them.

Here are seven basic rules of effective retainer agreements:

1. Retainers should *not* be for *labor* hours, rather hours of availability. This is access to your knowledge and experience. A retainer is about you being available to help others do their job, not doing it for them. As Saul Alinsky's Iron Law for consultants reads, "Don't ever do nothing for nobody that they can do for themselves." Always remember that you sit behind the pilot, not in the pilot's seat.

2. Retainers should spell out the details for the access to your knowledge. Ideally, this access is directly with the key decision makers. I recommend you insist that this access isn't for just anyone in the company.

3. Retainers should always be paid in full, in advance. Most retainers are for a period of one month, but also with a minimum

number of months committed. Make sure the retainer agreement states that you expect full payment for any given month to be made by the first of that month, and stick to your rule that your work for that month will not start until that payment has been made.

4. Know the difference between a retainer and a project. The latter is where you are much more actively involved and have sufficient control over the outcomes to provide more assurances. In a retainer, you are not guaranteeing anything with regards to results, just availability and advice.
5. Retainers are not cell phone contracts. If, at the end of a month, the client never called you or asked for any assistance, that does not mean they get their money back. You charged for being available, and you were.
6. Due to much of the above, retainers aren't normally the opening agreements for many consultants. They are a better fit for the end of more involved work (as extra support after you taught the staff how to do something, after you coached their leaders, etc.).
7. Retainers should be built around clearly defined and tangible objectives that start with the client's needs in mind, then build the retainer around meeting those needs. Even though you are not charging per hour, you should state a specific number of maximum hours the retainer would cover, and anything over that would need to be negotiated.

In general, retainers are incredibly valuable to both you and the client. They are effective revenue generating models and they overcome one of the more bothersome problems consultants have, which is dealing with inconsistent monthly income. Secure a handful of retainer clients and you know how much you will be making several months out instead of starting over at the beginning of each month wondering where the money will come from.

The other reason why retainers are so effective is because they are so profitable. Confused? What I mean is that profits are the derivative of number of hours worked for the revenue generated (ROI in other words). Very much like gym memberships, 80 percent of the companies paying for access to an expert on a retainer fail to actually use all of the hours available. In effect, you're paid for hours that were used elsewhere to generate more revenue. If they need you, that's wonderful, but you're not sitting around staring at the phone during that unused time.

Value-Based Fee Structures

Value-based fees take you out of a task-oriented relationship and move you to the most desirable relationship to be in with a client, in my opinion. In these kinds of structures your true value is tied directly to results the client gets out, not the effort you put in. Even if this is your objective in the previous kinds of structures, your means of charging the client is disingenuous to that intent with task-based models.

On my family crest, under our coat of arms, is the motto, "Facta Non Verba," which means "deeds not words." Unlike the previous task-based pricing models, these fee structures all walk the talk by tying consulting fees to actual results, not effort. In the end, the average business owner doesn't actually give a damn about how hard you worked, only what results they receive.

In value-based pricing you outline the scope of work you propose to your client in the exact same way as any pricing model, but when you give them your fee you give them one fee and one fee only. Preferably you will include all the tasks and materials you will provide in a bulleted list (e.g., training, coaching, teaching, investigating, meetings, reports, profiles, Ginsu knives, and the bamboo steamer), but you will *not* place a price on any single item in this list, ever. At the end of the proposal you give the client one price for everything. The items on the list aren't up for debate.

If you show price, you open yourself up to negotiations you don't want, like "If we take the personality profiles off, how much would that save us?" The answer to such a question would be, "Nothing because I'm not charging you anything for profiles. They are an important tool I need to deliver the overall objective, which *is* what I'm charging you for."

There are three primary kinds of value-based fee structures:

1. **Project-Based Fees:** Project-based fees are where you charge a single overall fee for the entire deliverable. One of the trickier aspects to this type of pricing is accurately projecting the amount of hours you will need to put in to deliver results. To be safe, when

you're new and not sure how long it will take you, calculate your best guestimate, then add at least an extra 30 percent to your estimate to cover overages.

Using the true hourly base rate, your task in this model is to break down all the things you will need to do to deliver the objectives. Determine how many hours it will take you to complete that work, multiply those hours times your true hourly base rate, and arrive at what you should consider charging your client. Even though you're using your true hourly rate, it is only for your purposes. Never share that with the client or report hours spent back to the client during the project, as it shouldn't matter to them in this model. Likewise, don't include hours to be worked in these proposals. You will work however many hours you need to make sure the objectives are met. The focus is on getting results, not what tasks you do to get there.

The following are points to make to the client as to why they want a project fee:

○ It always leaves the focus on results, not activity.
○ There is a cap on their investment. They know exactly what they will spend up front, no surprises.
○ There is never a "meter running." They do not have to worry what it will cost each time your help is requested.
○ It is unfair to place them in the position of making an investment decision every time they need help. They shouldn't have to make a budgetary approval decision before they ask you to handle some unforeseen problem.
○ It's very easy to judge what their return on investment will be compared to the cost of the problem.
○ This is the most uncomplicated way to work together. There will never be a debate about what is billable time (travel, report writing) or what should be done on site or off site.

2. **Contingency-Based Fees:** Unlike the project fee's fixed total price, contingency-based fees are where you make payment of your fee contingent upon some agreed upon goal or outcome. If you deliver the work in a project-based model, you get paid, regardless of the overall outcomes. With contingency-based fees, what you get paid depends on what results you deliver. While becoming more popular and definitely the most lucrative fee structure, in my opinion, this

can be one of the riskier ways to structure a deal and should be entered into very carefully.

There are two kinds of contingency-based fee structures:

a. *Set Reward Fees.* A "Set Reward" contingency fee is where you set a fixed price that you will be paid, but contingent upon results achieved. Example, you charge the client $15,000 to achieve a 5 percent increase in sales, $25,000 to achieve a 10 percent increase in sales, and $50,000 to reach a 15 percent increase in sales. At the end of the engagement you both determine what degree of objective was achieved, which will then determine your final pay. Because you will not be paid until you reach well-defined objectives, this has been called self-financed consulting by some, because your fees come out of the increased revenues you help deliver.

You will want to start by deciding how much the problem is costing the client. Then, determine a realistic objective and what you will have to do to achieve it (hours worked, materials, expenses, etc.) to come up with your total proposed fee, much like any other model. However, then you will need to break that overall objective into three or four pieces (e.g., 25, 50, 75, or 100 percent of overall objective) and tie your fees to results. If you deliver half the overall results, you will get paid half of your total fee. Make sense? The big difference between this and a project-based fee is that in this scenario you only get paid *after* you deliver, not up front.

b. *Set Percentile Fees.* A "Set Percentile" contingency fee is where you agree to take a percentage of the savings or new revenue you help the client achieve. For example, you help a sales company increase sales by 30 percent. In the proposal they agreed to pay you 25 percent of whatever new sales revenue you help them achieve, so since a 25 percent increase in sales would mean 1,000,000 new dollars in sales, you are owed $250,000 at the end of the engagement. I've even seen 50 percent of growth deals, where the consultant would have made $500,000 in this scenario. Unlike "Set Rewards," here you agree to one percentile, not compensation based on milestones met along the way.

Basically, a contingency-based fee is where you agree to not be paid until after the client receives their rewards, and you share in those rewards with them. It is the truest form of partnership and a model I think holds the greatest potential for the highest revenues; but with that potential for revenue comes equal risk as well.

The argument to the client is that they will never find a proposal with less risk. This is, in effect, a 100 percent commission-based structure. You eat what you kill. They get your expert services for nothing out of pocket up front. If you fail miserably, they pay nothing. If you win big and deliver tons of new revenue, you get to keep your fair share. Yes, there is still risk to the client in investing time and resources, but they will need to do that with whatever solution they decide on, so I consider it a wash.

Where this becomes sticky is if the client doesn't agree that you delivered 100 percent on the objective. Then you're left in a black hole of subjective definitions about who thinks what percentage has indeed been met, and what percentage of payment that justifies. And that can be a very ugly place to be! This is why it's only a good model to take when the results you will deliver are easily quantifiable (sales numbers, human turnover, reduction of costs, etc.).

It can work with things like leadership development or strategic planning or even executive coaching, but you must tie your fees to measurable outcomes of those leaders or processes, not intangibles like "They've improved as a leader dramatically." Feel free to provide any solution, but always tie your fees to the overall end results in the company that are absolutely measureable. That is either going to be money made, or money saved. Top or bottom line doesn't matter, just as long as those are the only two metrics you use to determine the success of your work or not.

Make sure you understand the pros and cons before risking either of them.

The Pros are:

○ *Self-belief.* Nothing tells the client how confident you are than being willing to share only in what you helped them kill. This is a true partnership. By doing this you are saying that you are partnering with them in perhaps the most complete way possible (risks and rewards).

○ *Significantly greater profits.* Due to those added risks you incur by partnering with the client, your consulting fees are normally 25 to 50 percent for flat fee contingency and 50 to 100 percent higher in percentile contingency fee plans.

This is decreased client risk. If you don't deliver as promised, the client hasn't wasted money. Moving payment to the end completely removes their financial risk.

The Cons are:

○ *You're not 100 percent in control.* The less you control the outcome, the less this model makes sense. For example, you train the salespeople, but you don't have any control over the installation teams that screw things up in the field. Sales don't increase because of poor installations, so you don't get paid because you weren't in control of all the important variables.

○ *Risk.* As a small consulting firm, the risk to you is very significant if you invest large amounts of time in something that fails to work, since you're placing all of your revenue eggs in one basket—at the very end of the project.

○ *Subjectivity.* If you fail to tie your results to tangible, quantifiable measures (sales, gross revenue, turnover) you risk having the client subjectively qualify your results, with no solid numbers to point to as proof of your benefit.

My recommendation: Tread very carefully into such deals with new clients or when you haven't delivered similar results to others previously. This usually is not a model for brand new consultants. It is a great model to aspire to, though, once you have more experience.

3. **Equity-Based Fees:** In the immortal words of the robot from *Lost in Space*, "Warning, Will Robinson! Warning!" For those of you not familiar with the 1960s TV series, the surrogate guardian robot (creatively named "Robot" by the way) warns the young Will Robinson in this way whenever he's in danger.

Equity-based fees are a form of contingency, and they act much the same as set reward contingency programs. The difference is that instead of cold hard cash you are paid with equity in the business. Like the young space-traveling Will Robinson, you could be in for great adventure with this structure, but equally in more danger than with any other structure.

Obviously the potential payoff is much larger than any one-time payment you could receive. If the company really takes off, then you would be part owner and your revenue could span many years.

Conversely, the potential payoff could be nil, because if the company doesn't take off you're left with nothing to show for all of your sweat equity.

In effect, an offer for equity in lieu of cash is almost always the client's idea to begin with. It almost always comes from a start-up company, and it almost always should be viewed as getting involved with another start-up other than your own. This is less of a business opportunity and more of an investment vehicle.

Be faithful to your first marriage and focus on generating revenue for that company, not investing valuable hours in some other company with the hopes that it will pay off down the road. As a new consultant/ business cash is king. Keep as much of it as you can until you're fat and profitable. Then you can consider making investments in other companies (or in the stock market for that matter).

My *strong recommendation*—wait a while on this one!

Thoughts on Pricing in General

- Being high is good! The perceived subconscious value of higher-priced goods or services is always greater.
- When you are just starting out, or hungry, it's easy to adopt a "will-take-all-comers" attitude. You wouldn't advise your clients to do this when hiring employees, so take your own advice and don't do it when you are hiring new clients.
- If price is their only objective, your outcome is doomed from the start!
- Know when to walk away. If you're hanging in with a difficult client who isn't worth the work you're putting in, get out. Don't stay with them because you feel for them. It won't do either of you any good.

Avoiding the Low Price Leader Trap

Too many consultants lower their fees in the hope that they will attract more clients. More often than not it's the newer consultant who does this, but by no means are they the only ones. There are lots of consultants wondering why their practice is not very profitable even after years of running it. The reason is that they have opted to be the low price leader, and they will never be very profitable.

Here's the flawed logic behind setting low prices:

- It will reduce barriers to entrance and bring in more customers.
- It reduces the odds I will get into tough price negotiations.
- Times are tough and something is better than nothing.
- Once I get them as a client I can increase their worth.

Here's the truth behind setting low prices:

- It only reduces the barriers to entrance for cheap clients.
- It increases the odds you will replace tough up-front price negotiations with even more difficult discussions about getting paid later on.
- Times are always tough—deal with it!
- Cheap clients will always be cheap clients.

Setting low prices can work to stay alive in true emergencies, or to establish your very first client base in order to show new clients you are a real business. It will never, however, be a viable long-term plan leading to significant profitability in this industry. You are not Walmart. Low prices attract clients who are only looking for the lowest-priced solution, which should tell you that they are more concerned with saving money than fixing the problem.

No matter how you spin it or what rational lies you make to yourself, when you lower your prices, you tell the clients you are less valuable. Don't do it!

How to Deal with People Who Always Want a Deal

Many consultants fail to fully appreciate that once you make a single concession on price, you've enabled a behavior that will inevitably cost you money and probably drive you crazy. Requests for price concessions generally emanate from the owners of small companies who are accustomed to haggling with everyone from the coffee vendor to the hourly employees (who, themselves, are constantly asked to lower their prices for customers), or from larger company purchasing departments and low-level buyers, whose ultimate responsibility is to spend less (not to deliver results, per se).

There are several keys here:

- **Never offer a price concession without a quid pro quo.** Once you lower fees (no matter how slightly) without changing the value of your offering, you create the bad kind of opportunity. The client will stick a lever in that slightly opened door and rip it off its hinges. Sometimes such concessions are the right thing to do, but never go into them lightly and always follow this rule: As price goes, so too does value. What this means is that you can take the price down 10 percent, but you must remove 10 percent of the deliverable at the same time—always. Example: "I can reduce the price by 10 percent, but I will have to take the four weekly calls down to three."
- **Negotiate terms instead of price.** If you feel it necessary to negotiate, start by negotiating the terms of the arrangement, not the price first. Giving the client a concession on the terms lets them feel as if they've won something, but you protect your margins and profits. Try offering more attractive terms for when they pay, or how they pay, not what they pay. Example: Take a look at the percentage you ask for up front or consider taking a percentage up front instead of 100 percent full payment.
- **Don't offer concessions first.** If the prospect is someone who wants a deal, then they will be sure to ask for it. Just don't be the consultant who brings them up first. Some consultants, feeling insecure about price, competition, or value, make the mistake of bringing up the topic of concessions. There's no need to create your own objections, or give them the impression you're insecure about what you're asking for.
- **Be prepared to deny the request and walk away.** Be confident in your value. We've had buyers whom we have interviewed tell us, "I always ask for a concession because I believe it's good business. I'm shocked at how often they're granted without any resistance, despite the fact that I'm seldom prepared to press the issue if I'm told no."
- **Make sure that ROI is always seen in dollars.** Whenever you are highlighting your value, it must be in hard financial terms. Telling a company that they will see "greatly improved performance" doesn't mean squat and has no connection with your actual price. However, telling them they will achieve a 10 percent increase in performance, which equates to $300,000 in new revenue for them, is making a strong case.

- **Always provide options, even to small businesses.** If the buyer says, "I love option three, but the fee seems a bit high," you should reply with, "That's why we have option two." (I cover this a lot more in Chapter 4.)
- **Stop work if you're not paid on time.** "Deal-seekers" are famous for delaying payments to squeeze out extra work. If you're not paid in advance, and a payment date has passed, allow 10 days and then stop working. Otherwise, you'll be in permanent debt to the company store. I can name two close consulting friends who both kept working too long after payment was "delayed" and both ended up never getting paid anything, each being owed over $20,000.

Proven Methods to Increase/Protect Your Profits

Here are a dozen additional tips on things you should constantly be monitoring as you build your practice, in order to protect and grow your profits.

1. **Sell them what they want, give them what they need:** As the consultant, many times we create our own problems by trying to convince the prospect that they are wrong about what they need, when in reality all we're doing is getting in our own way. Many times a client has a strong opinion about what the problem is and what needs to be done to fix it. It's a big mistake to try and convince the client they are wrong and sell them something else. A more effective approach is to agree to sell the client what they want in title, but deliver a program designed to address the real problem (i.e., what they need). I'm not saying you lie or deceive the client at all; rather you agree to deliver a solution to what they think the problem is, yet make sure you construct a solution that delivers more than just what they want, and cures the real problem. Example: I had a client who said "I will not pay for coaching, just leadership training," even though that's what his leaders needed. I wrote the proposal for "leadership training" but what I delivered amounted to coaching work with each leader. If this isn't an option, consider not taking them on as a client.
2. **Think long-term—real revenue is cumulative, not situational:** All truly large profits come from long-term relations with clients.

Remembering this is vital because when you realize that customer loyalty is the real payoff, you avoid making mistakes like getting greedy or making decisions based on short-term thinking.

3. **Ensure that the client is aware of the full range of your services:** It's amazing how many consultants fail to inform their clients of all the various ways they could assist their organizations. Sometimes it's simply that the consultant thought their client was aware, or figured if they needed help they would ask. Easy solution: Have a brochure that outlines all the different solutions or services you offer and make sure all of your clients receive a copy.

4. **Never turn away business:** There will be many times when you find yourself presented with an opportunity to provide services to your client that aren't your expertise. When this happens many consultants may make one of two mistakes. They either take on that business, not wanting to lose the money, but since they are not experts in that field they commit consultative malpractice. The second mistake often made is to turn that business down. Confused? The first mistake is pretty obvious and not something you should ever do. Putting your financial needs in front of the customers' is always a mistake. The second mistake, though, is that you missed an opportunity to be the organizer of solutions instead of the provider of them. Even though that specific work isn't something you can provide, that doesn't mean you can't go find another consultant who can partner with you to provide it. This isn't a referral, it's you contacting one of the consultants in your network who can do the work and inviting them to work "under your contract" rather than create their own. You don't want to say, "I can't help with that. Good luck," nor do you want to say, "I know a guy who does that, let me give you his number." What you should say is, "I don't specialize in that area but one of my *partners* does. Let me get him in here and let's see what *we* can do." Manage the solution for them.

5. **When asked prematurely about fees, just reply, "I don't know yet":** It's very common for clients to ask what it will cost to fix a problem, or how much you charge to deliver X, Y, or Z. Ninety-nine percent of the time they ask this question prematurely, before you've truly diagnosed the root of the problem. This is no different from asking your physician how much it will cost to fix your painful knee, ten minutes into your very first office visit. The best answer is,

"Well, I don't know yet because I don't know what the problem is. Let's figure out what the cause of your problem is first, then I will be glad to tell you what I think it will take to fix it."

6. **Do not accept troublesome or unpleasant clients:** *Warning!* No matter how hungry you are, no matter how desperate you are, do everything you can to avoid taking on troublesome clients. If you don't like them before they are even clients, how much do you think you will like them once you're actually working with them? I know this can be a very tough exception, and it requires discipline, but trust that in the end it is far worse to take on bad clients than it is to hold out for better ones. You will make much greater profits, in less time, working with the right clients.

7. **Seek out new business opportunities laterally during your projects:** Inside almost every engagement you will come across other problems that you couldn't see from the outside beforehand. While you're in the organization delivering what you initially agreed to, always be on the lookout for other problems to help out with. One of the paths the most profitable consultants take is expanding value laterally once inside, rather than selling similar value to brand new clients.

8. **Pro bono beats cheap every time:** It is far better to do something pro bono and protect value than to do it for a low fee and erode value perception. If I tell them something is worth $500 but the first one is half off, I just established a monetary value of $250 in their mind. If, however, I tell them it's $500 but the first one is free, then I haven't established any other monetary price points so that value is still $500. I know it sounds a little weird, but trust me it's true. The reason is that once I establish a discounted price, it's easier for a client to expect similar discounts. If I give the client one for free, though, no client would ever rationally expect all others to be free as well.

9. **Higher fees are always better:** Psychologically, higher fees create higher value in the buyer's mind. Granted, you don't want to price yourself out of business, but there can be no argument that all of the studies ever conducted consistently prove that the more something costs, the greater the value it contains in the mind of the prospective buyer. You should make it your job to be fully aware of what your competition is charging and make sure you stay in at least the top 25 percent of those prices, preferably in the top 10 percent.

10. **Value must include subjective as well as objective measures:** Since the majority of the buying decision is driven by emotional rather than rational influences, be sure to always incorporate human emotions, values, motivations, and reward in your proposals. Showing them how much money they will save or generate is important, but creating a vision of the positive emotional benefit is equally as important.

11. **Offer incentives for one-time, full payments up front:** Whenever possible, motivate your client to make a full payment in advance. Offer them a discount, or additional value. Money made today is far more valuable than money made tomorrow. You get rid of potential time wasted chasing payments down, and reduce the risk of not being paid at all. Let the money earn a return in your bank account, not the client's.

12. **It's always easier to sell new services to old clients than to sell old services to new clients:** Even though it's very important to always be adding new clients, don't leave any low-hanging fruit uncollected by failing to sell new solutions to existing or even old clients. You already have the relationship. You have already done all the hard work of establishing your reputation and garnering trust with these clients. Now all you have to do is walk straight to the front of the line and propose new services you didn't have before. Whenever you add any new service or product to your tool bag, always target existing clients first, then former clients, and only then brand new clients.

How to Increase Fees Appropriately

Consultants tend to make a huge deal out of this topic, and I'm not sure why. I think it's likely driven by fear and insecurity. If price is the only reason your client is doing business with you, you have a much bigger problem.

From time to time everyone needs to increase prices. Let's discuss the why, when, and how of increasing your fees effectively. There are various reasons why you should do this.

- **You underestimated time and effort.** You've delivered a specific solution enough times that you realize your original estimate of how long it would take you was short and you need to adjust price to adequately reflect the true time you put in on such work.

- **Your costs have increased.** You should never be the last stop on price increases. If your office rent goes up, you hire an assistant, your suppliers increase fees, cost of goods sold goes up, or there is even economic inflation, be sure to pass those increases along to your customers—unless you don't want to be profitable, that is.
- **Your aspirations have increased.** You decide you want to increase your annual revenue. Perhaps you started a little low and now that you're moving up you want to make X many more dollars next year. Perfectly acceptable.
- **Your "Who" or "What" has changed.** Sometimes consultants who started their practice offering broader services to a broader market decide to specialize in new niche offerings and to a more concentrated market. When you become more specialized you should increase fees. Becoming a bestselling author would be an example where your speaking fees nearly double or triple since your value just increased significantly.

The timing of increased fees is important. Here are the proper times for establishing the new fees, and some tips on how to go about making the increases.

- **New work.** If you've made a price increase, always add that to any new proposals from that day on, with existing as well as new clients.
- **Existing work.** Avoid increasing fees in the middle of an existing project if at all possible! You're pretty much stuck until you have the opportunity to make a new proposal for more work. The only exception that ever seems to be acceptable is if you have a very long-term contract and you can clearly demonstrate your increased costs. Even then, it's never a great move to change the rules in the middle of the game.
- **Decide what your increase will be.** Go back to the calculations you did on your true hourly base fee and adjust the specific factors behind your increase (e.g., increase your desired annual revenue, cost of goods sold, hours worked, etc.). Recalculate your true hourly base rate and then you will know what your new rates will need to be.

- **With existing clients.** If you absolutely must increase fees during an existing relationship, be sure to demonstrate the additional value you will be bringing to the table. The client won't really care that your rent went up, so either figure out how to show them how this will bring new value or don't raise your prices until that work ends. If you hire an assistant, show your client how doing so will benefit them.

- **Tell them live.** If you must increase fees with existing business, always inform existing clients of this in person. Don't ever increase the price of the next invoice and wait for them to find out and come back to you!

- **Expect drop-offs.** As you increase your value and fees, expect to lose a client or two. That's actually a good thing. This is an evolution and some clients will need to become extinct in that process. Their leaving just makes room for another client who sees you in your new value bracket.

4

How You Charge Is as Important as What You Charge

Proposals as Confirmation—Not Negotiation

There is a huge misconception about the purpose of a proposal in consulting. Many consultants view them as a "sales vehicle," which they never will be. Perhaps it's the consultant who hates negotiating, or sucks at selling or is perhaps just lazy—who knows—but the mistake is that they receive an inquiry from a prospective client and immediately send over a stock proposal that explains their services, what they will provide, and how much it will cost. Their hope is that the prospect will love what they see and either buy right then and there, or call them in to negotiate a final deal. The other equally misguided approach is to meet with a prospect, have a great discussion, and then, when the prospect asks, "What would you charge to provide this service?," you respond with, "Well, let me go crunch some numbers based on what you've told me, and put together a proposal and send it over." Either tactic is normally the kiss of death.

The only way a proposal should ever be used is as confirmation of what you and the prospect have already agreed to verbally or face-to-face. Here's your gauge to know if you're screwing up and using a proposal incorrectly. If your prospect has to learn the specifics of what will be delivered and how much it will cost by seeing it in the proposal for the first time, you're doing it wrong.

The right way to do it would be to discuss all of the deliverables with the client first, negotiate your proposal verbally, and arrive at an agreement. Only then should you draft a proposal and send it to them. Proposals are confirmation of what has already been agreed to, not a sales or negotiation vehicle.

The only exception to this rule might be a formal request for proposal (RFP) scenario, where the organization has to follow rigid rules for requesting multiple proposals from multiple vendors, and the only way you could join the running would be to do as they dictate. Large government contracts are almost always conducted this way. That said, my question to you would be, "Do you want to be just another vendor"? I wouldn't tell you to turn down a large contract, but whenever you are

83

hired as a vendor, you're a commodity and relegated to the ranks of "whoever provided the minimum we needed at the lowest price."

Such contracts are also the least secure, because the next consultant to come along with a lower price is likely to take that business away, since your greatest value proposition to such clients is just your price.

A good proposal has the following characteristics:

- **It is short.** Gone are the days of 20- to 30- page proposals. The big boys may still deliver them, but they are proposing immense million dollar engagements to corporations with a team of lawyers who stand at the ready to pour over such massive details. Keep them short (two to four pages) and to the point.
- **It is topic specific.** By this I mean drop the numerous pages of boilerplate advertising about who you are as a company, what you offer, testimonials from past clients, and any other sales material. If you use proposals as sales vehicles this makes sense, but you won't ever do that again. Since proposals are confirmation of a sale already mentally agreed to, don't bother selling the client in the proposal.
- **It covers expectations.** Be sure to include the specifics of who is responsible for what. Don't be vague here. Doing this helps avoid the contentious debates that can occur down the road when opinions about who was to do what differ.
- **It includes context.** When you write a proposal, include the titled sections below that focus on the context of the problem.
    - ○ **The Problem.** Restate the problem the client is suffering from and its literal impact on their organization (e.g., "Background: Acme Manufacturing is currently experiencing decreased sales costing $500,000").
    - ○ **The Cause.** Specifically state the cause behind the problem (e.g., "Cause: It has been determined that this decrease in sales is the result of ineffective hiring practices leading to poorly qualified sales staff, and poor management skills of existing sales managers.")
    - ○ **The Solution and Objectives.** Describe the overall approach you will take to correcting this problem and your overall objective in doing so (e.g., "IMX Consulting will work with hiring managers to identify the key traits of effective sales professionals and introduce the ability to measure for those in all new hiring

situations. The objective of this proposal is to increase sales by 50 percent in the first year, resulting in a $250,000 increase in sales.")

○ **The Specifics.** Under "the solution" I stick to the higher-level overview, not including many specifics. In this section of the proposal, I cover the tiny details. If you are careful to include the Who, How, What, Where, Why, and When, then you are covered.

Except for some of the minor details, all of these things should have already been discussed and agreed upon before you write the proposal.

A Brief Word on Contracts

Consulting contracts or service agreements are not something you should play around with. I won't say much here, because for your security I recommend you go to the experts on this one. Yes, you can go to someplace online like LegalZoom (www.legalzoom.com) and purchase a perfectly valid legal template to use with all of your clients, but you should also consider finding a good corporate attorney, as it's advisable to have a relationship with one anyway. The main reason this is very important is that you really need to protect yourself.

One of our independent consultant clients signed a deal with a big government organization not long ago. Due to a very bad contract, though, he ended up providing weekly training to a large government client every week for 52 straight weeks before he got paid one dime. It nearly cost him his business.

Even though it can cost a little up front, you really need a contract that represents your best interests. You're the one selling something, so the contract should be yours, not the client's. A protective contract should cover the following subjects.

- **Responsibilities (yours and the client's).** Confirm expectations across the board.
- **Compensation.** Nail the specifics of what, when, and how they will compensate you.
- **Confidentiality.** They may be exposed to your private information, and likewise.

- **Intellectual Property.** You worked hard to create unique offerings. You don't want your clients taking them and handing them to the corporate mother ship.
- **Liability/Indemnity.** You can't risk being involved in a lawsuit by one of their customers or clients because of their actions.
- **Equitable Relief.** What could you do if they try to screw you basically?

The Option of Multiple Yeses

Always give the prospect multiple options. Not giving options usually means you just increased your chances of not getting their business. Know any stores that sell one thing and one thing only? Giving people options allows them to feel in control, which always increases the odds that they will buy.

As you put your proposal together, give some thought to how you could create at least three different options. Most people like to choose the middle option of three. So make one lower-cost, one medium-cost, and one high-priced option for anything you offer. You can do that by starting with the highest-priced offering and working backwards, and then taking value off as you lower the price.

As you create these three levels, however, be sure to adjust value equally. Always add or subtract value along with price. By doing this you have given three "yeses" the prospect can choose from as opposed to just one. That's a 200 percent increase in your odds of getting the business. If you're offering coaching, the variables you might play with to create multiple options could be:

- Number of calls
- Length of calls
- Length of engagement
- Number of people being coached (e.g., group coaching versus one-on-one)

If you're offering training, the variables could be:

- Length
- Number of people
- Individual attention
- Tools

Get it? Almost anything you offer could be adapted to multiple options, but doing this is extremely helpful in getting more business. Just make sure that, as you create these levels, you don't create one that doesn't deliver real value to the client or pay you enough. You don't want to deliver ineffective loss-leader programs all month long.

The nice side effect of doing this is that you reduce the chances that you will get in a difficult negotiation with a client who wants a deal. With one option, they are free to ask for the same value but at a lower price. When you have another option below, it creates a blocking effect. This allows you to counter the request for lower cost with, "Well for that kind of price let's take a look at Option C." It's much harder for a client to rationally argue, "I like Option B best, but we want it at Option C price." How often do you think someone walks into a car dealership and asks if they can have the deluxe four-door model, but at the economy two-door price? There is a great deal of psychology behind having three options, and all of it has to do with protecting your profits.

Lastly, many times we're in a rush in a negotiation. It's on the fly, dynamic, and sometimes a little contentious. The last thing you want to do is be rushing to think in your head irrationally about what the best deal is, then find yourself standing in the parking lot going, "Damn, why did I agree to that"? When you create formal options, you do so in the calm of your office, alone, slowly and rationally. You ensure that each deal is optimal for you. Then, when you're in live negotiations, you can move to any one of these options knowing it is already well thought out and that it will be a good deal. This is why I say multiple options make the buyer feel they are in control. In reality, they are only choosing from options you're in control of already.

Negotiating Price for Maximum Profit

The number one key to effectively negotiating with your clients is to follow the proposal rules. If you've created a multitude of options (i.e., option of multiple yeses), then your negotiations will be much easier. If the client balks at the price of one option, find out how much they think they can afford and present one of the other existing options. As long as you stay within 10 percent of that set price, you should be fine. In this way, all you are really negotiating is which option is best, not the price of that option.

The second biggest tactic to effective negotiations is to give the buyer something that has great value to them but costs little or nothing to provide. If you're dealing with a client who fails to perceive the value of your offer, or just always wants to get a deal, having a cadre of services or products in your bag that add little to no cost to you is very valuable. The trick is that you tell the client its value in their benefit, not your actual cost.

Here are some examples from my own negotiations:

- I have an unlimited profile account that allows me to pay a flat license for unlimited talent profiles (hey, I own the company so it's one of the perks). My clients don't know this and assume each profile has a hard cost. In one negotiation I offered to increase the value of the offering by agreeing to provide free profiles for all their new hires for one year, instead of just their top two sales candidates. I told them the typical retail cost of those profiles, they told me how many people they interviewed in a given year, I multiplied those figures together, and they perceived a significant increase in the value of the proposal. It was a $50,000 contract to conduct leadership coaching for their sales managers. When I agreed to throw $15,000 worth of profiles into the deal for free, they were satisfied and signed the contract.

- In one negotiation I offered to increase value by adding free access to a video training library I had created on team building. This was a library of videos I had created some time before, and it was packed with lots of great value and information. It cost me nothing to include, but I was able to show it had a per-person value of $297. The end effect was not that I lowered the price of my proposal, but I raised the value of it in the client's mind by adding an extra $10,000 worth of value at no additional cost to the client. They perceived great value, but it didn't cost me a dime. We closed the deal.

The mistake here would be to add something that does cost you extra. In doing so you reduce your profit margins and you might as well not bother and just reduce the price on the existing offer, which is something you should always avoid doing.

Some of the general best practices in negotiations are:

- **Always be first.** There are two schools of thought as to whether it's better to let the customer be the first to state a price or you. Opinions vary and the business at hand makes a big difference as well. When negotiating your fees for consulting work, it is far better to be the one who states price first. Research actually shows that in such negotiations, when the seller is the first to place a price stake in the ground, the final outcome results in a higher price.
- **You're in charge.** You are in control, not the client. If you've followed the guidance in this book, you know what your true hourly rate needs to be to achieve your profit objectives. If the price you need is not what the client can afford, or fails to perceive the value, then they are more than likely not the right client for you. As an independent consultant you must remember that *you hire your clients*, not the other way around. If the fit isn't a good one, don't settle.
- **It's the offer, not the price.** If you've written a proposal with multiple options, and the price is a sticking point, then you're not offering the right solution. Shift to one of the other options. Remember, never adjust price without adjusting value. Buyers love to lower prices but hate to lower value.
- **Never negotiate with the non-decision maker.** Sometimes you can get caught negotiating with someone other than the true economic buyer (i.e., the one who actually signs the check). This is actually a buyer tactic, and if you've ever bought a car you've experienced it when the sales person, safely claiming they can't approve the final price, has to go to their manager for approval. Don't waste your time negotiating with someone who lacks the authority to approve the final check.
- **If it's contentious, you've probably already lost.** If you find yourself in some hot, emotional fight over price, you need to step back in your mind and ask yourself if you're in the right place with the right client. This isn't a negotiation between two warring companies or divorce attorneys. You should be on very positive terms with your client, both already on the same page as far as what needs to be done and how, and not witnessing any antagonism

whatsoever. Ask yourself, "If it's this damn hard to get engaged, how difficult will they be to work with once we're married?"

■ **Ranges are a waste of time.** Some consultants think it's good to put out a range of fees (e.g., "We're looking at somewhere in the ballpark of $10,000 to $15,000."). It's an absolute waste of time because you just set the bare minimum price you would be willing to accept, and that's all the buyer will see. If you feel you *must* use ranges, than just invert them. Make your ideal price the low end, and a price you would never expect to receive the high end. If they're going to lock onto the lowest price, make sure it's your optimal profit.

Invoicing Properly

Invoicing is something that should be done before you start delivering your consulting work. A big mistake many new consultants make is to land the business, deliver the business, and then deliver the invoice only after it's all said and done. Huge-O-mistake-O!

You never want to deliver value and then figure out if you're getting paid for it, or when. As a small business you don't have a receivables department. You can't afford to spend valuable revenue generating time chasing down what's owed you. Once it's out of the box and delivered, that's it. You can't call it back.

I'm not saying that most companies will try to screw you and not pay you, but it would be very naive to assume it never happens. If you didn't listen when I talked about never negotiating with the non-decision maker, you could find out that the person who authorizes the work failed to get final approval, and the CFO is saying, "I never approved this much, nor realized it would be X." Want to guess how many times I've seen consultants provide work to a client that then went bankrupt? Sometimes it's simply the case where you're working with a terribly disorganized firm that seems to always take 180 days to pay invoices, and now you're extending lines of credit.

Smart invoicing follows one rule: "Get paid before work is delivered." The only time it's acceptable to break this rule is if you're using one of the contingency-based pricing models we've discussed, and it's because those models break the rule that they are also the riskiest of all models.

If you divide your services up into phases, get paid for each phase beforehand. If the work doesn't break into phases easily, then just break the payment into phases unrelated to the deliverable (25 percent before day one; 25 percent 30 days out; 25 percent after 60 days; and 25 percent after 90 days). Just remember the rule, "No pay, no play." If at any point along that payment schedule payments stop, so too does your work.

A lot of you, especially the new ones, will balk at this because it feels unreasonable or pushy. You need to mitigate your risk. One failed payment for services rendered isn't the same as one item stolen off of a shelf in some huge store where the loss represents only a fraction of a percentage of their annual revenue. In your work, each and every engagement is a significant percentage of your year's revenue, thus potentially crippling you if the payment is not made.

Dealing with Deadbeats

First off, if you structure your payment cycle as described above, this shouldn't be a problem for you. From time to time, however, you will have clients who are late making a payment. First rule is "don't freak out." In most cases it's a simple mistake or oversight in processing the intended payment. I like to work from a four-tiered approach if I'm faced with this dilemma.

1. **Tier one:** Simply contact the client and inform them politely that they are behind on a payment. I recommend e-mailing the person responsible for paying you, so it's in writing. By person "responsible for payment" I don't mean the head of the company, rather I mean the person who cuts the checks in accounts payable, or in book-keeping. Normally this resolves the problem because usually it's a simple mistake. At this stage I may decide to continue delivering active work on my part.
2. **Tier two:** If I've e-mailed the client and still don't receive resolution in a day or two at most, then I move to making a call, but not to the person I e-mailed, but to the key person in charge of the project. (Note the change in targets here. During tier one I reach out to the employee who should have been instructed to cut the check. In tier two I reach out to the leader who authorized that person to pay me.)

I still want to approach the topic politely and may even add it to the end of another conversation, but it is a phone call, not an e-mail. At this point, however, I will hold up on delivering any more work until I get an assurance from the leadership in the company that they are resolving the issue. If I get that reassurance from the leader I may start working again, but if payment is not received immediately (within days) I move to tier three.

3. **Tier three:** If I am still not satisfied with the responses, I cease any and all work and call the most senior contact person I'm personally working with. By now we're probably talking about more than 7 to 10 days overdue, and I need to speak to the highest ranking person who brought me into the company. When I speak to that person I let them know that, since I've worked through the previous two steps and still haven't been paid, therefore I have to stop all work. Regardless of the circumstance, remember to be professional, since becoming angry and aggressive only makes you look the opposite, and it doesn't do any good. By stopping work, you've mitigated your exposure and effectively demonstrated that work will not start again until you've been paid in full up to date.

4. **Tier four:** If you reach this stage and still cannot get resolution, there is a two-stage process I recommend. By now you're well over 15 to 30 days or more out from when you should have been. First, have your attorney draft a polite but straightforward letter to the top executive of the company, informing them of the debt owed to you. You don't have to threaten anything through your attorney, just formally make the facts known in writing. It's amazing how a letter from an attorney makes some companies get the ball rolling. Second, if the letter from your attorney fails to work, your best alternative is to hand the debt over to a professional collection agency. Depending on the agency, they will either pay you a percentage of what they collect afterwards, or more frequently a percentage of what the debt is up front. At that point the debt is no longer owed to you; you've made some money (enough to cover expenses and a slim profit perhaps), and it is now someone else's problem. I've never had to go to this extreme, but it has to be included on this list, unfortunately, as I do know cases where it has happened. Of course, if I reach tier four, that client goes on my blacklist and I will never even consider doing business with them again.

Note: while the steps above will help resolve any problems you have with deadbeat clients, your greatest protection is to choose your clients carefully, structure your work so you are paid in full up front, or receive incremental payments before each stage starts, and ensure that you don't overextend yourself or become a lending agency. You can't control your client, but you can control your risk.

Firing Your Bottom 10 Percent

This topic has nothing to do with getting rid of bad clients or deadbeats, per se. It is strictly a technique used to increase profitability by ensuring that you're working only with the most profitable clients.

Wouldn't it make sense to work only with those clients who have the highest ROI for you? Your ROI should involve more than just monetary return, by the way. What I look for in the ROI includes satisfaction, enjoyment, excitement, challenge, and generating significant wealth. I strongly recommend that you create your own list of exactly what it is you want to get out of your relationship with your clients.

To ensure you're always getting a maximum ROI, once a year rank your clients based on how well they deliver in whatever specific categories you put on your ROI list. For my list, I use a 1-to-10 scale and jot down a score for each client, then put them in order based on the overall score.

Once you do this—and here's where I will lose a good deal of you—you want to identify the bottom 10 percent of that list and figure out how to tactfully let them go (i.e., fire them).

Right about now you might be thinking, "It would be stupid to walk away from any paying client." But think of it this way: that bottom 10 percent will be filled with the least rewarding, least enjoyable, least profitable clients. Granted, you might be one of the lucky ones and all your clients are terrific, but even if this is the case, there will always be a bottom 10 percent that returns the lowest ROI. Profitability is a game of efficiency. Unless you can find more hours in the day to work, your profits only increase as does your efficiency and ROI.

I'm not being Pollyannaish here. I know that sometimes grown-ups have to work hard even when they don't enjoy it. But one of the reasons you chose this career is because it gives you the control to decide which clients you work with, and which you don't.

If you do decide to let a client go, one technique I've found to be quite effective is to significantly increase their prices, in the same way John Butler did in the previous story. I don't have any problem actually firing a client, but there's no reason to be mean about it, burn any bridges, or be rude. Remember, your reputation will always be your reputation. I've found that doubling or tripling your prices with these clients achieves one of two things; either the client simply can't afford your prices and will have to stop working with you, or the client accepts your new prices and they move out of the bottom 10th percentile. Either way, the problem is solved.

Just imagine how much more efficient, profitable, and satisfied you could be by spending the time you invest in the bottom 10 percent with either new clients or existing ones higher up on the list.

Justifying Your Fees

One day a manufacturing plant stopped running. Somewhere in the convoluted maze of pipes, hoses, and pumps that was the main engine driving the line, something had stopped working. Try as the engineers might, they could not get the engine running again. When they called to inquire about buying a replacement engine, they learned it would take one week to arrive. As the company faced losing $50,000 per day for every day the line wasn't running, the GM quickly called a consultant who specialized in such things.

The next morning the consultant showed up and walked around the huge machine, eyeballing each and every part. After only 20 minutes of inspection, he pulled a piece of chalk out of his bag and made a big "X" on one specific junction point. Producing a large hammer from the same bag, he reeled back and slammed his hammer into this junction—at which point the engine sparked to life once again. He handed the GM his invoice and started to walk away.

The manager, having looked at the charge, exclaimed "You're charging me $50,000 for 20 minutes of work"? At hearing the disbelief and anger in the manager's voice, the consultant promptly spun around, took the invoice back, and revised it.

When he handed it back to the manager it read, "Chalk and hammer = $1.00, knowing where to place the X = $49,999."

The moral of the story is that you don't justify your fees based on time spent or the cost of the equipment and supplies you used. You justify your fees based on the benefit to the client. The consultant in our story got grief from a GM who failed to see the value properly. Whereas that GM saw time and effort, what the consultant really did was save them $300,000 by getting them up and running again seven days earlier. You could even argue that he saved them $375,000, since the replacement engine would have cost $75,000. Charging 14 percent of the problem would be fair in my book. Reverse that and you're talking about a return on your investment to the tune of roughly 700 percent!

The following are the critical aspects of positioning your fees that you must be aware of if you want to avoid the GM's response described earlier.

- **Fact finding:** As I will teach you later in the Diagnostic Sales Process, you will never be discussing fees until after you've already identified exactly what the problem is and how much it is costing the client in cold hard cash. The only good way to position fees is to be able to show the client their own statements of how much the problem is costing them. When a client has a 50 percent turnover in employees, and they tell me that each lost employee costs them $100,000 in training, productivity, and sales, and they are losing 100 people a year, that's an undeniable $10 million problem. When I propose reducing that turnover by half, I'm committing to an objective that will save them $5 million in real cash. If I were to charge them $500,000 for that solution, it would not be a very greedy thing or hard to justify. You can think in terms of, "Would you invest $10 to earn $90"? Basically, I've charged them a mere 10 percent of what I've delivered to them in real money (i.e., $5 million).
- **Avoid justifications:** You won't find success by getting defensive and justifying your fees. Explain them —yes. Justify them defensively—no. One of the most profitable consultants I ever had the pleasure of working with taught me that whenever one of his clients says, "Wow, that's expensive," he has learned to just say, "I know." He made sure not to be cocky about it, or pompous, but rather

confident and rational. If you've followed the logic in the previous point (fact finding), you shouldn't have to justify much because you're probably talking about charging roughly 10 percent of the financial value you deliver to the client, or even much less.

- **Comparative Reality:** The only thing that justifiably limits the value you should be charging (outside of your own insecurity or lack of confidence) is how your fees compare to the rest of the industry. You must consider what the market will bear. As the old saying goes, "Something is only worth what someone is willing to pay for it." You may find yourself looking at a rationally justifiable investment of only 10 percent, but if no client has ever paid that much before, you may have to consider reducing the price to an acceptable market level. Even though I argue that you should be considered one of the more (and maybe the most) expensive people in your field, if the 10 percent solution means you will charge $500,000, but the next closest consultant offers that same service for a flat fee of $10,000, you're too overpriced. Easy solution: Know what your competition charges, be in the very top range of those fees if you can, and calculate the 10 percent solution, but then cap it at just over what anyone else would charge.

5

Not Just Any Ole Fishing Hole Will Do

Choosing Your Target Market

Choosing who your future clients will be seems like an easy question to answer, but to prevent you from making a very common mistake it requires some upfront work on your part.

A lot of consultants start their practice and just skim over whom they will target by assuming they will sell to "anyone with a pulse." The more accurately you define your target clients, the better your chances are of finding them. Coming across as the generalist and trying to speak to everyone results in your speaking to no one, thus no one ever hears you.

Consider the following three variables when choosing your target market.

1. **Specialist versus generalist (why generalists generally lose):** When it comes to being the very best at something, rarity and exclusivity play a significant role. Basically, the more specialized you become the more profitable your practice will be. This isn't a new concept. More than 2,500 years ago Confucius saw the folly in trying to be too many things, when he said, "The person who chases two rabbits catches neither."

   We've all heard the old mantra, "You can't be all things to all people." The most successful and profitable consultants I've worked with are all specialists. Think about some of the professionals you know, such as doctors or lawyers. From purely a monetary perspective, in almost every single category of life or business, specialists significantly earn more than generalists at every turn. Being specialized benefits you by:
   ○ Making your marketing messages more accurate, more appealing, and more effective.
   ○ Giving you greater authority and credibility.
   ○ Allowing you to demand higher fees.

   Don't mistake my message here. I am not saying that you should specialize in one specific service or deliverable, rather you can deliver as broad a range of services as you want (e.g., leadership development, sales training, strategic planning, etc.), but deliver it to a small specialized group of markets (e.g., banking, legal practices, small manufacturing companies, restaurants, law enforcement, etc.).

Use your professional experience as your guide to which markets you should consider specializing in. Specializing your services brings with it added credibility ("I've spent X years in this industry"), and it also brings valuable experience that will benefit the client once you do get the business. You don't have to specialize in your prior industry by any means, but it does help jump-start your practice, since you can find clients faster and are already familiar with those waters.

2. **Selling Your Genius:** Another aspect of determining your ideal target lies in determining what you want to deliver first. To do this I seriously recommend you start by tying your greatest natural talents (your unique genius) to the services you offer. Doing so helps you deliver more effective results, at higher quality, with greater results and with more passion!

As you learned in "Myth of Strengths and Weaknesses" earlier in this book, you have certain natural talents. Just as learning your natural talents is a great benefit to you when it comes to crafting your role, such knowledge is equally as valuable when it comes to deciding what services you will offer.

I once had a discussion with a consultant whose natural talent was for anything but big-picture strategic thinking. He was a "right here, right now" myopic kind of guy who couldn't see any farther than the end of the street when it came to planning.

This guy went to a conference one day and met another consultant who was making tons of money by selling strategic planning to corporate clients. As soon as he heard this, the non-strategic consultant decided he too would offer strategic planning services to his clients.

His mistake was to assume he could read some books and learn how to help clients create strategic planning, even though he was no good at it. His results were horrible, his clients were disappointed, and he hated delivering the work. He failed to consider his own natural talents when it came to deciding what he would provide, and unfortunately he paid a dear price. As you begin to flesh out your list of offerings, be sure to stick to things you:

○ Enjoy—that align with what you love to do.

○ Have experience in—you should use your professional experience to build your expertise.

○ Are talented in—consider your natural talents and avoid offering services that rely on your weaknesses.

The temptation to deliver the hottest, highest priced services may be strong, but if you decide to deliver things that you yourself are not very talented in, you risk not getting great results and not being motivated to go to work each day.

3. **Differentiating yourself:** Differentiating yourself and standing out in a crowd is going to be vital if you hope to be profitable. Specializing is definitely one great way to differentiate yourself.

I imagine you've heard of Pareto's Principle. You may know it as the "80/20 rule" or the "Law of the Vital Few." Actually created by management consultant Joseph Juran, it's something you should be quite familiar with because it plays a role in your future profitability.

If you apply this principle to your market, you'll realize that approximately 80 percent of the money in consulting is going to roughly 20 percent of the consultants. Unless you want to be in the mass of 80 percent of the consultants who are fighting over the remaining 20 percent of the business to be had, you have to make sure you are one of those "vital few" Juran describes. To differentiate yourself from the competition, you have to be different. As obvious as that sounds, it is amazing how many consultants try to be just like all the rest in the profession. Specializing is a great way to achieve that differentiation, and here are some other ways you can achieve it.

○ **Voicemails.** You don't have to have a goofy recording. Try returning the call within one hour. Now *that's* different! Many times I find myself chasing the actual person I want to hire.

○ **Follow up.** Try sending a handwritten thank-you note after meeting someone for the first time.

○ **Smooth contact.** Make sure you are super easy to get in touch with. Consider providing your cell phone number, or use an answering service so your client never gets a voicemail. I know one consultant who uses an answering service that operates 24/7, so no matter where his client is, he or she can reach a human and leave a message. Now *that's* really different.

○ **Deliver better service.** One of the best ways to differentiate yourself is through the client experience. When your clients experience a superior level of service, great results, and satisfaction, you do a lot more than just differentiating yourself.

○ **Your brand.** Don't shoot for a logo or brand that looks and sounds just like everyone else in the marketplace.

○ **Pricing.** This can happen by being more expensive than most of the competition (which is different), but it can also happen by using one of the contingency fee structures I've already discussed. Sharing the risk and being paid only after you deliver results is still quite new in this industry, and therefore different.

○ **Collaterals.** See what you can do to make your brochures different. I know a few consultants who use business cards that have slightly different shapes (rounded corners, or a bi-fold business card).

The only thing I would warn against is that in trying to be different you can sometimes go too far and become, well . . . weird. Seek to be different, not bizarre.

And don't forget that being "better" is the best form of being different. Ask yourself how you can deliver better value, better service, or better solutions.

The Greatest Profit Key in the World

One of the greatest profit-driving lessons I've ever learned—ever—is to separate yourself from your profits. My way of describing this lesson is to: "Stop trading your time for their money!"

If all of your deliverables involve your actually delivering them, you severely limit your ability to increase profits. Since there are only so many hours in the day, such revenue generating strategies leave you with only two options. You can either work more hours, or you can charge more.

If you provide coaching services, then when you're not on the phone coaching clients, you're not generating revenue. If you provide training, when you're not in front of the room actually training, you're not generating revenue. If you provide strategic planning, goal setting, conflict resolution, problem solving, or any other consulting service that requires you to be physically present (live or virtually), when you are not doing these things you are not generating revenue, and thus you are limiting your profitability.

In order to break this bind that holds you and unleash greater profits, you have to figure out how to provide value to your customers *without* actually having to be there to deliver it personally. The most profitable consultants achieve this separation by adding another stream of revenue known as "residual passive income streams."

A residual and passive income stream means you are providing value to your clients, but not delivering it yourself. This is how you generate revenue while you're on vacation, sleeping, playing with your kids, or spending your time marketing and prospecting for even more business. Yes, delivering actual value yourself will always be a good portion of what you do in your business, but don't make it the *only* way.

I recommend you achieve this feat of separation by using what I call the DTS model. DTS stands for "Do it. Teach it. Support it," and here is how it works. With everything you deliver, consider how you could:

- **Deliver it—yourself.** The first time that you deliver a service, do it yourself. This delivers immediate results at the hands of the expert. Of these three steps, here is where you charge the highest amount.
- **Teach it—to them.** The second time your client needs the same service, offer to teach it to their existing staff. This doesn't work for every service or every client, but if it makes sense, consider teaching the client how to do what you do. Here you charge pretty much the same as doing it yourself, but position it as a train-the-trainer situation, where you're transferring valuable knowledge that will live on forever inside the client organization.
- **Support it—with them.** Once you've taught the company how to do something, support it through either an ongoing retainer for support, coaching those who are now delivering, or—the best way—is to build something disposable into the program you teach (e.g., a psychometric profile or a license to use your training materials). Here you charge the least but spend the least amount

of time, and it's perpetual income for you that is passive (i.e., you aren't spending time delivering it).

Let's use an example from my own consulting work. I provide leadership training as one of my services. Here's how DTS works for me.

Step #1: A client hires me to conduct leadership development on their senior leaders. The first time I work with that client I deliver the training myself. I collect my fees and I could be done but, knowing that true profitability comes from repeat business, I present the client with the opportunity to have me transfer this piece of my expertise to someone inside of their business. They will always have leaders, and new leaders will come on board. Instead of hiring me to come back again next year—instead of having new leaders wait until the next year's training—why not acquire that knowledge for themselves, so that it becomes part of their organization and can be used whenever they need it without paying for an external consultant again?

Step #2: My client, seeing the rationale in acquiring such knowledge for themselves and saving money in the end, agrees, and so we select the right staff member or members to become "certified" in my leadership training program. I deliver a train-the-trainer program and charge them a fee that is similar to what I charged for the first program. The key to this model is that I've built a leadership talent profile as an integral part of this program. You can't complete the process without this profile. It is a "disposable," because each person receives one link to complete their profile online, and once they complete it, that link dies. Any new participants in the program will need their own new link.

Step #3: The "Support It" phase is the real jewel and ultimate objective of this model. Since I'm trying to figure out how to make money while I'm not there, I sell an unlimited license to that client for access to those profiles. What that charge is varies depending on the size of the client, but it is typically somewhere between $1,000 and $5,000 a month. And, after the first month or two I *may* spend as much as two hours a month supporting the internal staff on how to debrief these profiles. Stack 10 such support contracts on top of each other, at $1,000 per, and you just achieved $10,000.00 a month in residual income (or $100,000 a year), all for roughly 24 hours of work a year! See what I mean?

Here are some of the various things I've seen work in the DTS model.

- **Profiles.** Any kind of personality profile or assessment can be built into the actual program (I will give you a comprehensive list of where you can access these kinds of tools in Chapter 8).
- **Rights of Use licenses.** Allowing your client to have unlimited use of your training program and materials. Give them the source materials so they can print however many they want, and they pay you a monthly or annual fee for those rights.
- **Coaching retainer.** You could charge a monthly retainer for the ability of their new trainers to have direct access to you for coaching; or, you could agree to audit one class per month. This might also include something along the lines of hosting one group call a month to coach trainers, and then reporting to leadership how they are doing.
- **Video Libraries.** Put together a resource library of simple videos and license access to it to your client. In Chapter 6 (under video marketing), I will show you how incredibly simple it is to actually create such videos. Be smart and target the largest swath of employees in the company. Create a library for customer service, sales, teamwork, management, supervisory, and so on. Create four to six or more separate videos in each and charge monthly or annual fees to allow the client unrestricted access to this training library.

The DTS model can work very well for a wide variety of services you deliver. It's up to you to decide if what you provide could be effectively taught to someone else. There will be a mix of things you either don't want to include, or can't include, in this model.

I hear you asking that most common question: "Does this really work? If I teach them how to do what I do, am I not working my way out of more business?" As I said, for some things you provide you may not want to offer this as an option. However, instead of looking at it as killing future business, you have to look at this as a way to continue to

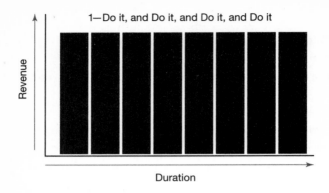

Figure 5.1   The Typical Consultant Model

generate revenue—*without being the one who delivers it physically!* If you build a practice where you *are* the business, you must consider you will never have an exit strategy because the day you stop showing up to work is the day you stop making money.

Here's a visual to help explain why this model is so powerful. Figure 5.1 above depicts the typical consultant model of "I am the deliverable."

In this scenario you should achieve higher per engagement fees, but that situation eventually ends (the work and the revenue). Because you're tied up delivering revenue, there's little to no time for prospecting or keeping your sales funnel full.

In the DTS model (Figure 5.2) you structure your engagement with a client so that your physical hours worked taper off to a bare minimum, yet you retain a stream of revenue indefinitely.

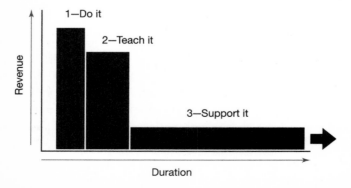

Figure 5.2   The DTS Model

By doing so you create revenue that lives on even after you've left the building. With that free time you avoid the dreaded curse so many other consultants suffer from, where you find either feast or famine. When you spend all of your time delivering work, you have no time to make new sales calls. When that work ends, you have a sales funnel that is empty, and you have to start from scratch. Meanwhile you make no money. I call it "cyclical hell."

With a DTS approach, though, you establish a client that will continue to generate nice revenue even after you leave to go find more of the same. Figure 5.3 shows just how significant this extra time can be, and you can imagine what you could do to grow your business with all this extra time.

Lastly, over time you stack multiple support clients on top of each other. The cumulative effect of having just 5 to 10 support clients (each paying even as little as $500 a month) could be generating $5,000 a month in passive and residual income each and every single month (see Figure 5.4).

So to the question of, "Does this really work?" I personally can testify to the effectiveness. In my own business I've built a network of 750 clients who pay me a flat monthly fee to have access to these kinds of tools. I work to support each of them but I have it down to a science now. These clients pay somewhere between $300 and $1,000 *a month*, so you can do the math and understand how this model built a seven-figure practice for me.

Trust me . . . it works!

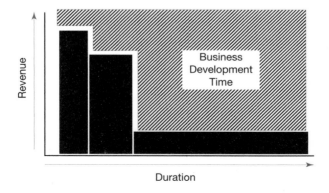

Figure 5.3 Business Development Time

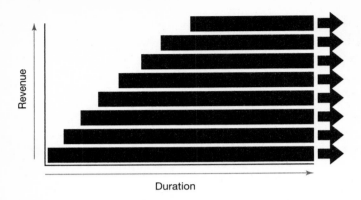

Figure 5.4   The Cumulative Effect of Stacking Multiple Support Clients

Team Separation

There is one other way to separate yourself from revenue. This approach is where you build a team of consultants who deliver the actual work for you.

If you either create partnerships with other independent consultants, or become large enough to actually hire a team to deliver consulting solutions, you can sell consulting engagements that are delivered by someone else on your team. You spend your time hunting and gathering business, outsource someone else to fulfill it, and keep 25 to 30 percent as manager and for sales commissions.

With independent consultants you normally would retain about 25 to 30 percent of the gross; as subcontracted consultants you would expect roughly 70 cents on the dollar. If you're using straight employees you may be able to keep closer to 45 to 50 percent, but the cost of employing them will equal roughly the difference in what you keep, so it's a wash. Either way you earn a healthy percentage of the business, without being the one who delivers it.

As I said, you don't get off scot-free, as you still need to do the heavy lifting of landing the contract, managing the consultant who delivers the work, and handling the invoicing and collection of fees. However, it is a very effective way of generating revenue while you're out doing more sales and marketing . . . or sipping a cool drink on a beach somewhere.

In my experience, I've found other consultants are very open to this model because the majority of consultants aren't very good at selling, and they are more than happy to take 70 percent of an engagement if all they have to do is show up and do what they love to do.

Just so we're straight, though, this isn't a referral. You are signing the contract with the organization, and then another contract with consultants to provide services in your name, under your brand, on your contract. They aren't allowed to sell more services once inside. They must run all critical decisions past you. Abuse these laws and they are fired. Be sure to include a non-compete clause in your contract with outsourced consultants.

While not for everyone, it's definitely a model to consider. I know consultants who have built a team of 10 such "partners" and they have a seven-figure practice, a true legacy business, and act more like the CEO of a consulting company than the sole entrepreneur.

What Is Your Final Offering (UVP)?

Now it's time to wrap everything that is your story into what is called a Unique Value Proposition (UVP). This is also sometimes called the Unique Selling Proposition, or Unique Selling Point. A Unique Value Proposition is a promise of the value you will deliver to clients. In its marketing version it is normally a single statement that captures the essence of your company, and it states:

- What value you promise to deliver.
- Who you promise to deliver it to.
- How it is unique, special, and sexy.

It starts out as an internal document that you complete in order to make sure you have the strongest proposition. At the core of any strong UVP will live one thing and one thing only: how your company will improve the overall condition of your client's organization. Everything else in your UVP will either point to or support that singular cause. Don't make your UVP what you think is awesome, novel, or special unless you're sure your customer would agree. Be sure to select only the most powerful benefits because it needs to be fairly concise. Steer clear of cluttering it with minor features, functions, and benefits, especially the ones that are not unique to you. Here are the two ways to build your own Unique Value Proposition:

1. Grab the rough draft mission statement you created in Chapter 1.
2. Then answer these questions:
   a. Who is your target market? (Remember the specialization work you've already done in this book; make it niched and targeted.)
   b. How do you benefit the client the most? (Recall your genius, talents, experience, expertise, and passions.)
   c. How are you unique? (Go back to the work you did under "differentiating yourself" to highlight how you are different.)
   d. Can you prove or guarantee it? (If you offer any guarantee, include it here.)

Once you're created a powerful UVP that captures your greatest benefit to the client, now it's time to take it to your clients by writing your Unique Value Proposition Statement. This is the short, sweet, and unique version of your overall UVP. Some examples of great UVP statements are:

- Domino's Pizza: "Delivered to your door in 30 minutes—or you don't pay"
- Google: "Find what you want—quicker"
- Amazon: "Low price, wide selection, anytime, anywhere"
- BMW: "The ultimate driving machine"
- Walmart: "Everyday low prices"

Of course, these companies have spent billions on branding, so they can get away with shorter UVPs because everyone already knows what they do. For unestablished companies, like yours, you will need to educate the prospect a little more on what you offer and to whom.

With your polished UVP ready to make an impact, it's now time to integrate it into everything you do. From your website, to advertisements, to your elevator pitch, to every last piece of marketing collateral, your UVP statement should fully describe your business.

6

Seek Only to Give—Marketing That Actually Works

Effective Marketing

Here's where the real fun begins. I'll admit that so far I've covered what some might consider the mundane, or beginner, aspects of building a profitable practice. Granted that without the things you've just learned your practice will be in jeopardy, but they are still rather, shall we say, fundamental.

We're about to enter into some seriously different topics, ones that run counter to much of the conventional wisdom. For the rest of this book I'm going to cover sales and marketing in ways you've probably never considered before. These approaches may be surprising at first or completely different from what you *thought* you should do. Get ready to let go of any outdated beliefs you may hold about how consultants grow their practices, and get ready to do some real work!

By now you've built your practice, you know who you want to sell what to, and for how much. Now you just have to kick off a marketing program that actually works. Since aggressive marketing tactics aren't very well accepted in this industry, you need to think more like the physicians or attorneys you know when it comes to marketing and business development. To understand how to market, you need to first understand what type of marketing you need.

Education-Based Marketing

There are really only two broad categories of marketing: sales-based marketing, in which you take on the role of a salesperson and deliver a sales message, and education-based marketing, in which you take on the role of an expert or thought-leader, and educate prospects about their problems.

Sales-based marketing is built around a sales message or sales pitch. This pitch is delivered using methods that reach out to prospective customers, such as telephone selling, direct mail, and door-to-door sales. Marketing experts like Seth Godin and Donny Deutsch call these kinds of activities *interruption-based marketing*, because they interrupt people. They also talk about how the market is becoming way too savvy and inundated with such interruptions, and their effectiveness is decreasing rapidly. Did you know that the average response rate for direct mailings has dropped below 0.5 percent? Simply put, interruption-based marketing is *dead*! Don't bother. Don't do it, Due to its timely demise, I will not be talking about sales-based marketing at all in this book.

Education-based marketing (EBM) is built around an educational message instead of the old sales pitch. The educational message is delivered to prospective clients through educational means. These include written materials, publicity, advertising, seminars, webinars, podcasts, blogs, websites, and videos.

Sales-based marketing creates the following problems:

■ Clients go out of their way to avoid you because they are tired of being sold to and sales-pressured. A basic tenet of buyer psychology is that you have to give before you receive. You can't be successful simply by asking to receive with sales pitches.
■ Clients don't think they can trust you because you immediately position yourself as a "salesperson" associated with all the other perceptions of salespeople (true or otherwise).
■ Clients are defensive and protective because they expect you to try to pressure them into buying something they don't want or need.

EBM provides the following solutions:

■ You give clients what they want (i.e., information and advice), and you remove what they don't want (i.e., sales pressure).
■ You establish yourself as an authority, a reliable source of information.
■ You don't seek out clients; instead, they are induced to seek you out.
■ You reach clients during the first stage of the decision-making process, often before they call your competitors.
■ You receive calls from clients who are genuinely interested in your services and you screen out people who are not real clients.
■ You begin to earn your prospect's loyalty because you've made a concerted effort to give, not receive.

Now you understand why the American Marketing Association featured this innovative method on the front page of its national publication, *Marketing News*. When done properly, education-based marketing is the most effective way to grow your consulting practice. When butchered, however, it can do you just as much harm as good.

The Golden Rules of EBM

Following are the three biggest rules I've learned when it comes to doing it right. Take these lessons to heart and you will avoid being butchered.

EBM Rule #1

In order to effectively use EBM to grow your business, there is one incontrovertible, inexplicable, unavoidable law that must *never* be broken: "Seek to educate—not to sell."

This is easier said than done. You will have to undo years of programming, which has taught you that you must pitch your wares and close prospects. Simply put, the moment you do this, you have moved from education-based marketing to sales-based marketing. Doing so will close the door on that prospect because nothing reinforces the image of the slick salesperson like hiding sales pitches in educational gift wrapping. If you promote an educational event, provide 15 minutes of bland, obvious, and easily available content as your "educational" message, then switch to pushing registration for your upcoming leadership boot camp, you die.

Another thing that is difficult for some to grasp is that when you deliver education, you give it away for free. Many old-school advisors will tell you to talk *about* the solution, but not "give it away" or the prospective client won't need you anymore. If you follow this path and try something like, "The solution to this problem involves specialized training. Here at Acme Consulting we've developed the best training methods in the industry and for just $999 you too can solve this problem," then your education-based message just became another sales pitch . . . and, again, you die. Nothing pisses your prospect off more than feeling like they were misled into thinking you were going to educate them, then given the old bait and switch.

Here's an example of a program I did with Tony Robbins. Please go to the following website (http://bit.ly/dqerR9). I want to share this site with you because it is a great example of the power in giving education-based content away. Feel free to watch the videos if you want, but the main things to see are the comments below each video. What I want to stress is that all of these comments are from prospective clients, not existing clients. These are people I've never met. Can you imagine prospects reacting this way to a marketing brochure or a sales pitch? Here's just a sample of some of the more powerful statements from prospects.

- "Hey, great video. . . . Never thought about this and really looking forward for the next videos, can't wait for them." (Note how the prospective clients have become excited about watching more—are they being pulled?)
- "I think this concept is brilliant because it makes so much sense. I have already started to spread the word." (Forget being pulled; now they are helping pull others virally for me.)
- "Smart and successful entrepreneurs offer something for free to attract traffic to their sites and increase sales, but you did something more, Jay. You gave out a piece of yourself with the sincere intention of serving others. At least, that's what I received out of your whole project (the videos, the assessments, the worksheets, your articles, your ideas, everything). Just price-less!" (Just an example of how well EBM works when done sincerely.)
- "I genuinely think that you and Tony Robbins may have saved my life. I have spent this whole Christmas week watching all the videos, doing the tests, and listening/watching." (Some things go beyond a discussion of profitability. Here we achieved the consultant's mission of improving the client's overall condition.)

I can hear you asking, "This is all great, but what good is it if you give everything away"? Watch the fourth video in this series, and you'll see where I do make a sales offer. And I've sold high six-figures off this fourth page, by the way! Depending on when you read this, that final offer might be as low as $47 for an e-course, or as high as $4,000 for a three-hour coaching program.

Remember, you are not educating them on what your company can do for them. You are actually giving them actionable content they can use tomorrow to improve some aspect of their life. The more unique, easy-to-apply and effective that content is, the more valuable an expert you become.

EBM Rule #2

You don't get paid for telling someone what to do. You get paid for actually showing them how to do it. While you want to truly educate your market, the whole purpose is to get them to pay you to help them do what you are telling them to do. As Dr. Marshall Goldsmith says, "All the leaders I coach read the same articles, they listen to the same thought leaders, and they all have access to the same educational content. Where I make my living is in the fact that it's not about understanding the practice of leadership—it's about learning how to practice that understanding."

Marshall practices this same education-based approach because he knows that his clients don't need him to educate them on what to do, just help them do it. Your clients are the exact same. Any one of them can buy one of the thousands of books on management theory and practice. They can attend Harvard and Yale management or leadership courses online. Where they need your help is in saving them the time it would take to become the expert, plus the experience in how to actually apply that knowledge.

When it comes to EBM, rule #2 is: "You give away knowledge—but you charge to help apply it."

EBM Rule #3

Own the blood bank. There's an old, albeit morbid, quote that says, "I just want to own the blood bank in a time of crisis." In other words, you want to control the supply when demand is at its highest. Your objective in your EBM is to create a significant demand for something you control. Examples can be for a very specific set of developmental steps, or proprietary profiles that measure valuable talents.

Example #1: If your topic were "The core competencies of effective leadership," then being able to actually measure those competencies would become of vital importance to your audience. You would want to highlight those specific competencies in your educational message. You just gave away valuable knowledge, but you also just created demand for the ability to actually measure those competencies.

Example #2: If your topic is "The keys to building customer loyalty," then having a structured process to train and develop such loyalty would become vital to your audience. You would want to highlight those specific steps, and any proprietary materials, in the body of your educational message. At the same time you are giving away the knowledge that a company needs to engender trust, hire caring types, reduce touch points, and invest in new technology, you aren't actually telling them how to engender trust or hire "caring types." You've just given away more valuable knowledge, but you also just created demand for how to actually do what you said.

To help you create your own education-based marketing messages, I've included an EBM Creation Guide for you in Appendix B.

The 16 Marketing Vehicles

Now that you understand why you should use EBM marketing, let's learn the different marketing vehicles you can choose from to actually get that education-based message out to your target audience.

No one of these vehicles will suffice all by itself. To build a truly profitable practice you need to be using as many of these as you can. In the military we called it force multipliers (i.e., attributes or factors that greatly enhance your existing abilities and odds of success). Using a multitude of these vehicles will deliver the same advantage to your practice's bottom line. Regardless of the vehicles you choose, there are some basic concepts to always follow for effective education-based marketing:

- **Be prolific:** Whatever you do, do lots of it. Do it consistently and prolifically. A common mistake consultants make is to start with a flurry of activity, then stall and assume old stale marketing will continue to drive new results.

- **Repurpose:** Repurposing is the practice of taking one education-based message and turning it into another vehicle. If you need an article and a video, don't write a new piece for each. Instead I will show you how to take the first article and turn it into a movie, so you take advantage of the work you've already done.

The 16 marketing vehicles are:

1. Social media marketing
2. Blog marketing
3. Article marketing
4. Lecture marketing
5. Webinar marketing
6. Video marketing
7. Presentation marketing
8. Podcast marketing
9. Workshop marketing
10. Book marketing
11. Drip marketing
12. Referral marketing
13. Partnership marketing
14. Network marketing
15. Research-based marketing
16. Press release marketing

For more education on any of these vehicles, visit www.The ProfitableConsultant.com.

Website Marketing

Technically, website marketing isn't included as one of the 16 marketing vehicles because it's less a "vehicle" and more the solid home base for all of your other marketing vehicles. The site in and of itself serves as the hub, from which all of your other marketing efforts emanate. Yes, it's important to have it listed with directories and formatted properly, as I discussed in Chapter 2, but your website's greatest power will come through all of the other vehicles pointing back to that home base.

To accomplish that, the one very important thing you must do in all your marketing efforts is to create a back link to your awesome website. A back link is simply a link back to your own website. Somewhere in every vehicle you will put a link that leads back to your website. Don't put more than one, since some places you will publish these vehicles frown on too many. All you have to do is to write your website somewhere inside that article, video, or presentation. When you do this, be sure to place HTTP:// in front of your website address so search engines can see it is a URL link. Example: "HTTP://www.innermetrix.com."

This one simple act will drive traffic back to your main website, and raise your standing in search engine findings. The more back links your website has, the more the search engines will like your site, and the more they like it the more people they will show it to.

Think of your main website as living at the center of all your marketing efforts, as illustrated in Figure 6.1. When visualized like this I

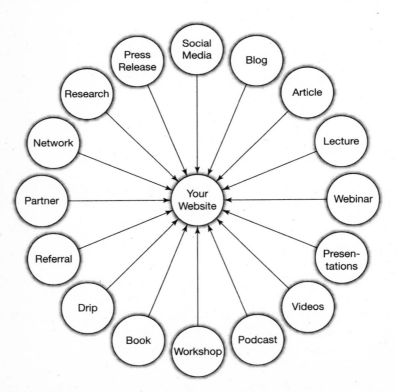

Figure 6.1   Your Website—The Center of Your Marketing Efforts

think it's easy to see why most consultants' websites fail to help them generate any real business; they create only the center (i.e., the website itself) and wonder why no one ever comes by. Fortunately this won't be you because I will show you how to fill these vehicles easily, and with as little effort as possible, and drive massive traffic back to your site—filled with all sorts of great leads.

Social Media Marketing

In Chapter 2 you learned how to set up your social media sites. Now it's time to start using them! In its infancy, your social media strategy will have little or no followers, but don't worry about it. Step by step, through the activities given to you here, you will start to see those numbers grow. You just have to be patient, which I know can be hard when you're hungry. The three things to do are:

1. **Get Oriented:** Log into your social media accounts and start learning. Everything is there from tutorials to help buttons. It isn't rocket science, but you do need to play around to learn how to use each site. Get in there and start learning how other people are using it. Also make sure you complete your profile as completely as possible as this is a key to growing a network later. Side note: If I could only use one social media site, absolutely hands down it would be LinkedIn, because it is the most business oriented and has returned more leads for our consultants than any other site.

2. **Reach Out and Connect:** Once you're comfortable with the specifics of using each site, it's time to start growing your network. At this point you're in the toddler years. Learn to crawl before you try to run. Start slowly building your network by finding some old friends and inviting them to join your network. Find interesting groups to join, or that are relevant to your market. Find people who have similar interests such as alumni, former business colleagues, and personal friends, and invite them to join your network (hint: use the "People You May Know" feature in LinkedIn). One of the reasons it's important to complete your profile is because the site will refer you to people you may know based on where you've worked, associations, schools, even hobbies or geography. Find Facebook fan pages of businesses you know, places you go,

campaigns or causes you champion—and join them. As you do this, don't try to go from three friends to 3,000 overnight. Some sites will actually prevent you from requesting to connect with too many people at one time, but it isn't good practice anyway.

3. **Interact . . . Politely:** Once you've joined some groups, get involved. I can't stress the importance of this enough! Your sole objective is to develop a network of connections and position yourself as an authority. You do not do this by using social networks to sell anything. Joining a bunch of sites and spamming the hell out of them with one-directional sales posts is a surefire way to make people drop you like a hot potato. You must interact, and do so with topics already posted by other existing members. I recommend you spend at least two weeks (minimum) just reading and commenting on what others have written, before you start your own new thread. People see how long you've been online, and there is an unwritten rule that you have to earn your place before you start pontificating. Certain groups like the one I own on LinkedIn, "The Association of Independent Business Consultants" (which should be one of the first groups you join) won't allow newbies to post in the first several days. Get to know before you start to get known. A great thing to do is to also post links to someone else's work. If you read an article that is germane to one of your groups, copy the URL to that article and post it on your social media outlets. Just be sure to give proper attribution. Becoming the authority doesn't have to always rely on your own authority.

Frequency of Posts

There are those who will tell you that you should be making three or four tweets, two or three LinkedIn comments, and one or two Facebook comments every single day. I will *not* be one of those people. I mean if you're one who can do this level of interaction online, I'm not going to tell you to stop. However, I would warn you about spending too much time online. You will never build a profitable practice from behind the safety and comfort of your computer screen! As powerful and important as social media and online marketing will be to your success, there is also a significant risk to never getting out in the real world and shaking hands and kissing babies.

A more realistic frequency of posts would be once per day on each medium. That would mean you log into LinkedIn, Facebook, and Twitter once a day each. Have a look around, see what you can add value to in the way of discussions, and make a comment or two. A great feature of all of these sites is that you can be e-mailed or notified whenever a topic you're involved in receives a comment from someone else. Every thread is witnessed by thousands of others, perhaps tens of thousands given the size of some of these groups, so keep the conversation going and the relationships building.

You have to be careful, though. It's unbelievably easy to suck up quality revenue generating time by spending all your time in front of the computer. Social media is a good thing, but too much of it is a very bad thing. Don't allow yourself to get pulled into the fray a hundred times a day. Compartmentalize your social media time to rigid blocks of time, and stick to them.

Let me correct a misconception just in case it exists. Social media is *not* a sales marketplace. It is a networking place. We haven't discussed networking in depth yet, but you never ever sell anything at a networking event. Not only does it not work, but it's also "not good form" as our London office is prone to say. The rules in social networking are no different.

What social media outlets *are* for is to create a large network of like-minded people. Many of them could definitely become clients, but not inside the social media machine. To benefit from social media you will create a large network of people, become known to that network as an authority, and then induce them to come to you when they have any needs.

Blog Marketing

Welcome to the blog-o-sphere! As with your website and social media outlets, earlier in the book you set up your blog. Now it's time to learn how to use it.

Why is blogging so important in the first place? Because, as I've been preaching, education-based marketing is the most effective way to market in this profession; and, one of the best ways to do that is to write! You don't need to be the next Hemingway but you do need to publish authoritative information on the topics you specialize in. Blogging is one of the most effective ways to get that educational message out. It's fast (most blogs are short); it's networked (people register for blogs and it grows virally); it's in line with the education-based mentality (blogs are education or opinion based); and it's popular (over 375 million people read blogs every month, compared to only 39 million who read newspapers).

One of the best parts of blogging is that it is very time-efficient. Unlike any other form of marketing, blogging is much less formal and requires much less time. The blogging community grew out of what were at first online diaries. The word grew from the original "web logging." As such, blogs are informal, casual, and short. Let's dig into some of the basics of what constitutes a good blog:

1. **Solid content:** Granted this can be subjective, but there are two core aspects almost everyone agrees on:
   - **Usefulness:** Sites like Twitter and others suffer from a plethora of mind-numbingly useless content. Much of what is shared is of no use to anyone in the world, including the writer. I coined the term "Social Needia" some years back as a way to describe the inane and useless content many people post online, in some desperate *need* just to be listened to ("Please look at me"!). In order for any blog to be successful it has to be useful to your target audience. To ensure your content is useful, follow this rule: "Always start with what the customer wants, then give it to them." Before you chose a blog topic, make sure you ask yourself, "Would my target audience find this useful"?
   - **Uniqueness:** Warning, there are a lot of bloggers out there. Ensuring that you stand apart from the masses requires that your voice is unique. Bloggers who write about the same damn topic as everyone else, in the same damn way, may have "useful" content but zero readers because their posts are no different from everyone else's. To be unique means that you write in a very different voice, or style, than everyone else. The best way to make sure you are doing this is to research what others are blogging about in your niche. Go read what other blogs have to say to the same audience. I don't necessarily care how you make yourself different; just make yourself different. Another aspect to help you stand out is to speak to a very specific niche. If there are too many

blogs talking to business owners, write to owners of one niche of business (e.g., banking, law firms, electronics).

2. **Length:** There are two kinds of posts: lead and follow-on. Lead articles lead the way. They are normally the first articles you write on a given topic or category. As such, they are typically longer and more comprehensive. Follow-on articles are relevant to the lead article, but more like a sub-story of the lead article and shorter. Ideally your lead blog posts should be around 500 to 1,000 words long, while your follow-on articles are normally smaller at roughly 300 to 500 words. The primary factors affected by the length of your post are:

   ○ **Attention span:** The average web reader can take as little as two minutes maximum to stop by a blog. No, that's not a typo. The average time your typical reader will spend checking out your entire blog post is *under 120 seconds!* As a result you *must* keep your blogs short, sweet, and power-packed.

   ○ **Less equals more, literally:** When it comes to having your blog found on Internet searches, quantity is definitely a factor. Joseph Stalin was purported to have said, "Quantity has a quality all its own." In this context you can take that to mean a greater number of shorter posts has greater value than a smaller number of longer posts. Granted, each post should be complete in and of itself (I hate "Continued in part II"), but you can create stand-alone sound bites that are short, thorough, and interesting, and create an entire family of them.

   ○ **SEO:** There is some pretty strong supporting evidence that blog posts in the 300- to 500-word range rank better, which is exactly what you want if you are to attract new readers. So, while you may create lead posts to get a new topic rolling, try to stick with more follow-on articles.

3. **Scanner friendly:** Break it up, make it visually diverse, use **bold**, CAPS, <u>underlines</u>, and *italics* more frequently then you would in a normal article. Don't go overboard either, of course. Use bullet lists as well. Spread out your words a little more than you normally would and make good use of short paragraphs with lead headings. Lastly, use images! Humorous ones are even better.

4. **Reader friendly:** Sometimes I come across a consultant who likes writing at a post-graduate level, but because people are scanning they simply don't have time for complicated writing. In any

marketing, you want to avoid fancy words or anything that would score above 30 in Scrabble. Ninth-grade reading level, folks!

5. **Granular:** Inside your blog you have the ability to create categories. For those worried about alienating target audiences by limiting their topics to too narrow a field, you can create categories for either industries (e.g., banking, manufacturing, law enforcement) or for different solutions (e.g., sales training, team building, hiring). This allows you to write blog posts that are very specific to a niche market, but still speak to a wider audience through your other categories.

Visually, you can imagine your blogs as similar to Figure 6.2, with your main blog, subniche lead articles, and then subspecific follow-on articles under each of those.

6. **Titles are king:** When it comes to choosing the title for your specific blog posts, I really can't stress enough how important they are. Not only do they help differentiate your material, but the search engines that will help channel readers to them rely heavily on the title as well. It has to be unique, and it has to be explanatory. Search Google for any word or phrase you want and see just how few words you can actually see in each result. Sure, you see a ton of titles, but look at how few actually mean something.

Not only do properly crafted titles help grab the attention of the search engines, but they grab the attention of the reader. "Becoming a better leader" is a title that will get lost among the masses, and

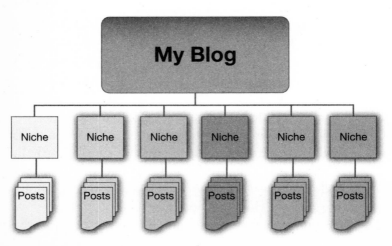

Figure 6.2   Your Blog's Hierarchy

it will not tell your prospect nearly enough specifics about what you are offering them. "Why So Many Banking Leaders Suck," on the other hand, stands out, is definitely different, and is specific to one of your niche audiences.

Some specific keys to writing effective blog post titles are:

○ **Keep them short:** Under 40 characters is ideal. Too long and the search engines may penalize you, or worse yet, the entire title doesn't appear in the search results so the reader can't read all of what might be an awesome title.

○ **Grab the reader's attention:** Stand apart from what others are posting in your field. Controversy, shock, even confusion are some tactics, but just be careful that your content lives up to your title. The title, "The World's Greatest Cure for Turnover!" will be seen as hyperbole and not very believable. Calling your article, "The Shocking Truth Behind Law Firm Revenue," is more justifiable, assuming you actually have some startling facts.

○ **Speak to a need:** Try to always include the "niche and need" in your titles. Titles like, "Small Manufacturers Are Crazy for Turnover" not only talks to leaders of manufacturing firms, it also lets them know you're addressing a specific need (with only 36 characters to boot).

○ **Keywords:** The keywords you use in your title play a significant role in maximizing the potential size of your readership. The same Google Keyword Search Tool you used when selecting key tags for your website (https://adwords.google.com/o/KeywordTool) is a tremendous resource to help determine the effectiveness of the titles for your blog posts as well. Last month I used this tool to help me avoid a mistake in titling my article about customer loyalty. When I used the keyword *tool* and entered "Customer Loyalty," which was the title I really wanted because it spoke to what the true objective should be, I found out that 950,000 people searched "Customer Loyalty" in the previous month. When I entered "Customer Service", though, I learned that 9,500,000 people searched for that. Even though I wanted to preach about the importance of focusing on loyalty rather than service, had I titled it Customer Loyalty I would have only reached one-tenth as many potential readers. My solution was to choose a title of, "How Customer Service Kills Customer Loyalty" (and in just 38 characters—giddy up).

7. **Be interactive:** Don't make the mistake of working hard to draw the attention of prospective clients, only to ignore them once you get that attention. Blogs should not be thought of as fancy marketing brochures. They are a great way to bring prospects to you, where you then interact with them! Just like LinkedIn, most blog programs are set up to automatically notify you whenever someone comments on one of your posts. Elicit comments as well. Don't preach to them, ask for questions and comments. Being interactive builds the relationship, and people like to do business with people they know and are comfortable with.

8. **Be consistent:** You must be consistent. You may only choose to write one article per week, or one per day, but the key is to be consistent. Not only will your readers develop a habit of looking forward to your next topic, but search engines also like consistency, and your rankings will be higher as a result.

9. **Pace yourself:** Like anything else, blogging won't return new readers overnight, let alone new clients. Building a large subscriber list to your blog takes time, so be patient. It's not unlike most other forms of marketing. The old rule is "seven touches" or someone has to see your name seven times before they actually pay attention to you. What's true of print and other forms of marketing is mostly true online as well. The medium might be new, but the psychology of the human using it isn't.

How to Grow Your Blog Tribe

Here are the top 10 tips to build a large and loyal following of blog readers. They are listed in the order in which you should complete them:

1. **Write your first five lead articles:** Get these written and posted within the first week or two of opening your blog.

2. **Be prolific:** Write a follow-on post at least once a week, preferably more. These are 250 words long and simple to write when you are feeding off the lead post you started with. As your tribe grows you won't have to be as prolific, and you will spend more time in discussions with readers on existing posts.

3. **Spread the wealth:** Don't hoard your expertise on your blog. Comment on other people's relevant blogs, but do so in an education-based mind-set, not a marketing one. Never hijack someone else's blog.

4. **Scratch backs:** Be sure to reference other posts you've read that are relevant and provide links to that blog (make sure to also give credit attribution). Don't approach this with a scarcity mind-set and worry about sending prospects to the competition. Share links to other blogs that aren't direct competition, but more importantly to content that would be interesting and helpful to your readers.

5. **Repeat:** Go back and write more lead articles, more follow-on posts, and keep attracting comments. By repeating this process, and monitoring old posts, you will soon build your own tribe of followers, wherein you will find prospective clients who already see you as an authority even before you speak with them.

6. **Submit your blog:** There are numerous blog submission sites where you can submit (i.e., register) your blog and the site will list it for all of their viewers to find. These sites draw a lot of viewers. You only submit your actual blog site once and you're done. I'm telling you to register them now instead of when you first set your blog up because you should have some posts on your site when you submit it. Here's all that I would consider registering with. The more the merrier:

Best of the Web Blog Search

Bloggeries

EatonWeb Blog Directory

OnToplist.com

Blogged.com

Blog Search Engine

Blog Catalog

Globe of Blogs

Blog Universe

Bigger Blogs

Bloggernity

Bloggapedia

Spillbean

Blogging Fusion

Blogflux

Bloglisting

Blogio

Blog Digger

Blog Pulse

Technorati's Blog Directory

Blogarama

Blog Hints

Blogtopsites

Force Multiplier alert: When you post any blog articles, share a link to it on all of your other social media outlets.

Article Marketing

Writing articles is a crazy effective way to establish your authority and drive traffic to your site. I bring it up right after blog marketing because I find it's easier to write a blog first. Once I've done that I can take that blog and expand on it, flesh it out a little more into an article of 750 to 1,000 words, keeping the same title. Follow the same EBM rules about not selling. This is repurposing.

Since your article needs to be more formal and longer than a blog, give it some structure that doesn't normally exist in a blog post. I recommend you address the following four items in your article, and in this exact order:

1. **The Problem**—Write about a specific problem you know to exist for a large percentage of your target audience.
2. **The Cause**—Once you've defined the problem, explain what causes it. You're the authority. Speak from that expertise as to the primary cause, or causes, of that problem.
3. **The Solution**—Give the reader the solution. What works best is to couch that solution in terms of, "What the best performing companies in the industry do differently is . . . " or "What those companies I've worked with who do not suffer from this problem do to prevent it is. . . . " This turns you into more of an authority speaking on a subject than someone trying to sell something. Think third party, objective, unbiased, and not as someone with an agenda.
4. **Lastly, add an "About the Author" block**—At the end of each article you should have a very concise block of text that acts as a mini-bio. Similar to what you see in another journalist's articles, include something to the effect of, "John Dough is a regular contributor to multiple leadership sites and is a management consultant specializing in Botswanian basket weaving workshops. He can be reached at (e-mail and phone)."

Submitting your article is the big thing you must do. Writing it doesn't help if only 50 people read it. You can submit your article to "article submission sites," which are these way cool sites that aggregate articles on all sorts of topics. These sites do a lot of work to draw large volumes of readers, and sort articles by category so those readers can find what they're interested in easily.

Some of these sites require you to register an account the first time, but all other submissions are simple, fast, and painless. Unlike blog registry sites, you need to submit each new article you write. The more of these you submit to every time the better,

www.ezinearticles.com

www.squidoo.com

www.hubpages.com

www.maximumarticles.com

www.goarticles.com

www.articledashboard.com

www.contentdesk.com

www.articlesbase.com

www.isnare.com

www.selfgrowth.com

www.articletrader.com

www.buzzle.com

www.articlecity.com

www.articlesfactory.com

www.ideamarketers.com

www.articlealley.com

www.web-source.net

www.articlecube.com

www.promotionworld.com

www.selfseo.com

www.articlesphere.com

www.amazines.com

www.businessknowhow.com

www.excellentguide.com

Force Multiplier alert: When you submit any article anywhere, post a link to it on all of your social media outlets.

Lecture/Seminar Marketing

If you've written a blog and then turned it into an article, why not keep the momentum and turn it into a speech? You should easily be able to turn a 1,000-word article into a 45- to 60-minute lecture. See how repurposing starts to make your life easier? You don't want to write a whole new speech from scratch. Take the tiny blog, which grew to an article, and now make it a speech.

Where can you go to give this speech? Contact all the local member organizations—Chambers of Commerce, professional trade groups, associations, or anyplace else where your target audience congregates.

As part of their corporate charter, associations are expected to provide value to their members, and they are constantly looking for new educational content. Offer to speak as an expert on some topic at their next event, or schedule a dedicated event yourself in partnership with one of them.

You can create a speaking business if you like. Consider joining Toastmasters (www.toastmasters.org) and The National Speaker's Association (www.nsaspeaker.org). Just know that you don't have to become the world's greatest speaker for our purposes here. Speaking, in this instance, is only a means to an end.

That end is being seen as an authority, and speaking is a great vehicle for communicating that authority and building that credibility. This means you can create your own speaking platform too. Consider putting on virtual webinars or teleseminars. Find where your target market lives, listens, or congregates and figure out how you can find a way to speak in front of them (on and offline).

Just as with your blog or article, don't deviate from the education-based marketing plan. Don't make your speech about you, your services, or your products. Don't take the last five minutes to throw a sales pitch at the audience. You're not selling as you speak, you are establishing credibility. Do, however, be sure to give all attendees a packet that contains the printed article you've built your lecture from, your business card, and perhaps some brochures about your company.

Try to record a video of your speeches whenever possible. Once you're very comfortable with revenue you can hire a professional company to do that, but it's quite expensive. Many times the venue or association where you're speaking will be recording the speech for you, so be sure to ask for a high definition copy.

The good news is that you can do it yourself if you have to, and still get good quality for not a lot of money. There are wonderful HD video cameras out there anywhere from $150 to $2,000 for a very well equipped professional version (e.g., Sony NXCam). Yes, you can spend tens of thousands for a camera, but don't. Have someone man the camera on a tripod and you're good to go. If you're going to do it yourself I would also recommend you purchase a wireless lapel microphone for somewhere around $150, but it's not absolutely necessary in the very beginning.

Force Multiplier alert: When you schedule a speech, announce it on all of your social media outlets.

Webinar Marketing

A webinar is simply a seminar conducted over the web. As such, it is not any different from what I just covered in seminar marketing. Same thing —delivered virtually. Most of the same rules of seminar marketing apply to webinars as well (e.g., topic, size, fee or free, length, call to action, etc.). By conducting your seminar virtually as a webinar you gain some significant benefits, though.

Being virtual, the number of attendees normally grows substantially because participants don't have to travel or incur any expenses to benefit from your message. They can stop what they are doing at work and instantly be online attending your webinar. Most webinar software allows you to record video and audio so you can turn your webinar into a movie to add to your education library with one click of a button. And, your costs to conduct the webinar drop to almost nothing compared to a seminar.

There are a couple of downsides to webinars, however. You don't get the personal interaction you might at a seminar. Webinars are normally never longer than one hour, so they might be shorter than what you would deliver in a live seminar. Exercises and activities don't work well in the virtual medium of a webinar either.

In all, I very strongly recommend webinars as one of the most effective, least cost prohibitive, and fastest ways to grow your marketing base. Note I said grow your base, not your revenue, because we're still talking about marketing here—not selling. Given the services you provide webinars make poor sales vehicles. That's okay, though, because like all of the other marketing vehicles, they are designed to help establish yourself in your market, make your prospects aware of who you are and what you offer, position you as the expert in a specific area or areas, and induce the prospect to come to you. In our industry sales happen face to face. The objective of marketing is to effectively get more face time with more people—to then sell to live.

To conduct a webinar all you need to do is sign up with one of the numerous webinar service providers in the marketplace. While not quite as prolific as Internet service providers, it seems they are close at times. The ones I recommend are:

■ GoTowebinar (www.gotomeeting.com)
■ WebEx (www.webex.com)

Both of these providers offer low-price solutions to create your own account, allowing you to conduct both webinars and teleseminars (i.e., webinars without pictures). On a side note you won't find a seventeenth marketing vehicle in this book dedicated to teleseminars because they're passé nowadays. Why limit your interactions to strictly voice when for the exact same cost, time, and ease you could share a slide presentation?

To get started, register an account and start playing around. The interfaces are very intuitive and I recommend you practice with at least one friend to make sure you understand how it works, since there's nothing worse than showing up in front of 20 prospects online only to find you don't know how to operate the system. One very nice feature of both of these webinar providers is that they give you a fully managed registration system. This allows you to create a new webinar, give it a title and some nice descriptive copy, and generate a unique link or code that allows anyone to register automatically. These systems then give you a list of all those who have attended, along with their e-mails, so you can do some premarketing.

In either system you will conduct the webinar as the host and will have the ability to speak, show slides on your computer screen, mute or unmute any other participant (in small groups you might decide to let members talk freely), pass control to someone else who might be co-hosting with you, and lots of other cool features. Participants can ask questions, which you can see, or raise their hand if you've decided to go the route of unmuting one person at a time to allow them to ask their question to the entire group. Too many features to mention here, but all of them help ensure you deliver a high-quality educational message that solidifies your authority in the minds of your prospects.

Some keys to conducting effective webinars are:

■ **Send reminder e-mails:** At three days out, the day before and the morning of, send reminder e-mails to those who have registered.

- **Start early:** I always log into the webinar system at least 15 minutes in advance (earlier if you're new to the system), just to make sure everything is working properly. If possible, have someone else dial in as a participant just to make sure both sides are working.

- **Provide ground rules:** Right after your introductions let the audience know some basic housekeeping specifics. For example, how will you take questions (i.e., raise your hand and I will call on you, type them in and I will get to them as they come up, or save them all until the end). Let them know they are muted to keep the line clear for all to hear better. If you plan to record the webinar let them know so, and if you plan to make it available and how.

- **Burn the script:** Don't assume that simply because no one can see you that it's okay to read from a script. True, it is easier to use notes in a webinar but steer clear of reading verbatim as it comes across very badly in how you sound. Be casual, have fun, and seek to be interactive and engaging.

- **Be Socratic:** In the very beginning tell them what you will be talking about, then tell them in the body of the webinar, and at the end summarize what you just told them.

- **Sprinkle calls to action:** I've found that if I am going to give the audience a call to action at the end (which I always do, of course), I get much higher response rates if I mention the fact that I will be giving it to them about one-third of the way into the webinar, again two thirds in, and then actually give it to them at the very end.

- **Show clear and simple presentations:** There can be lag times in what you see on your screen and what the participants see, depending on the quality of the Internet connection on their end. Keep your presentation slides neat, simple, uncluttered, and brighter rather than darker.

- **Respect their time:** Are there times where I blew past my one-hour time limit? Lots! However, I always make sure I fit the entirety of my core content into the time I said I would take so if anyone has to leave due to other things on their schedule they don't miss out. If I stay long I always let the audience know, at the end time, that we've covered all the core material and anything from here is just in response to questions. It's also good to let them know that you're recording this and will send the video out in case they miss anything.

- **Have a call to action:** By now in this book you should know what I'm going to say. If you're not going to make a solid, easy, and compelling call to action, why bother?
- **E-mail the video or slides:** On any system, for anyone who conducts webinars, you will never have 100 percent actual attendance from those who registered. For some it's because they registered last week and now just don't have time. On average you should expect roughly 25 to 40 percent as a benchmark attendance level. I've had plenty of webinars where we reached 95 percent, but it's more rare. So, to get the most bang for your buck, share the recording of your webinar with everyone who registered, regardless of whether they made it or not.
- **Repurpose:** Since you have a video recording of your webinar, why not share it with as many people as you can. Post it on your website in an "Executive Education" library of sorts.

It bears repeating. I personally think webinars are perhaps the single most effective means of marketing for our industry for all the reasons I've stated above. If you want to start growing now, start creating your first webinar now!

Presentation Marketing

Don't stop now. Since you more than likely created a presentation to show with your speech, why not repurpose that work as well. Take your presentation and share it with the world. As silly as this may sound, presentations aren't normally the best way to *present* information. They are better at supporting your presentation as you speak. However, if you organize them well enough they can be yet another good way to get your message in front of prospective clients.

There are a growing number of websites where you can post presentations online so anyone in the world can see them. Just like your blog or article submission site, these sites are searchable by all search engines, and allow anyone on the Internet to find your presentation. There's nothing better than prospective clients watching some education-filled presentation that brands your company all over their brain, all while you are sleeping.

Follow all the same guidelines for choosing titles and keywords, but there are some specific guidelines for presentations you should also follow.

Since this presentation will be seen without your explanation, you may want to go back through your presentation and make sure each slide makes sense without you explaining it. As you do so, be sure to stick to these universal rules of effective presentations:

- No more than four bullets per slide.
- No more than 40 words per slide.
- No more than 8 to 10 sentences per slide.
- Keep font size 24 or larger.
- Make them visually dynamic (use images as well as words).
- Animations are ideal, but simple beats fancy.
- Proofread, proofread, and proofread.

Once your presentation is ready to go, consider uploading it to sites like these:

www.slideshare.net

www.empressr.com

www.authorstream.com

www.brainshark.com

www.knoodle.com

www.powershow.com

www.slideboom.com

www.show.zoho.com

www.slideroll.com

www.slideworld.com

www.vuvox.com

www.slideshow.com

www.slidesix.com

Force Multiplier alert: Whenever you post any presentation to any online sharing site, post a link to that presentation on all of your social media outlets.

Video Marketing

I talked briefly about video recordings of your live presentations, but that's not the only kind of video you can turn into a marketing vehicle. Take that same presentation you just made and turn it into a video too. Video marketing is another very powerful form of marketing. In fact, it's quickly becoming one of the most effective with the popularity of YouTube or iTunes. Search engines love videos.

Both PowerPoint (PC users) and Keynote (Mac users) allow you to do this very easily by recording your voice as you click through the presentation; then it will be exported as a video for you. Post this video on your YouTube account and Google makes it searchable by the 7 billion people on the planet now. Here's how to do it:

- Start with the presentation from your speech, or make one for your article or blog if you don't speak.
- Run to your local office supply store and pick up an inexpensive (roughly $20) microphone to plug into your computer's USB port. You don't need high-end quality, but the built-in microphone on your laptop is a little too low-end as well. My favorite, anything from Blue Microphones (www.bluemic.com). Their Snowball and Yeti series are great, and cost from $65 to $150.
- If you're using PowerPoint for PC:
  - Open your presentation with your microphone connected to the computer.
  - Click "Slide Show" on the top bar.
  - Click "Record Slideshow."
  - Speak into your microphone, while walking through each slide as if you were presenting it to a live audience. PowerPoint is recording your voice and the timing of the slides as you do.
  - Click "File" and "Save as Movie" and the software will turn it into a movie file for you.
- If you're using Keynote for Mac:
  - Open your presentation with your microphone connected to the computer.
  - Click "Play" on the top bar.
  - Click "Record Slideshow."
  - Speak and walk through each slide just as you would with PowerPoint.
  - Click "File" then "Export" then select "Quicktime Movie" and the software will turn it into a movie file for you.

Once you've created your movie, upload it to your YouTube account. You can also upload it as a video podcast to iTunes. Remember to follow all of the same guidelines for naming, keywords, EBM, and so on. The ideal target length for such videos is under 10 minutes, so you're not talking about a ton of work here. I recommend you link to them from your blog on your website as well.

Remember earlier when I talked about creating a video library that you could license to your clients to create residual passive income? This is the exact same technique you would use to build such a library. The big difference is that the videos you license would be much longer than 10 minutes, but you get the picture. Create a library of topics, create a presentation for each, and turn them into movies and license access to them. Talk with your web developer for ideas on how to create this virtual library and licensing access.

Force Multiplier alert: Whenever you post any videos online, share links to it on all of your social media outlets.

Audio Podcast Marketing

In keeping with the spirit of repurposing, you can also turn your movie into a podcast. The term "podcast" is a combination of "broadcast" and "iPod." Basically, it is content broadcasted over the Internet and listened to on any MP3 player (Apple or otherwise).

What are they good for? Well, depending on your age you may remember driving around listening to books on cassette tapes or CDs (I intentionally left 8-tracks out. Some things should just not be remembered). For years businesspeople have been listening to educational content on the go. Today's business owners are no different, but the format is a digital file called MP3 and it's played on iPods, smartphones, laptops, or tablet devices. Just imagine putting your content out there for prospects to be listening to the next time they are flying on a plane somewhere. If you title it well and get it out, they just might.

There are a couple of ways you can go about this. You could either record your voice reading one of your articles or presentations, or you could even record yourself interviewing another person (or vice versa) in more of a talk-radio-style approach. The important thing is that you are penetrating the audio podcast world with your education-based messages as well.

To make a podcast you have the option of learning how to do it yourself, or use the automated software that most podcast hosting sites provide for you. If you decide to go it alone, you will need to download the following things:

- **Audacity software:** Download the free program that will allow you to create MP3 files, Google "Audacity," and download the software program and install it on your computer.
- **An MP3 Encoder:** At the same site where you downloaded Audacity, download "LAME MP3 encoder," which allows Audacity to save your recordings as MP3 files.
- **A podcast hosting site:** See list of recommended hosting sites below.

Once you download Audacity, install it and become familiar with how to record your own voice and save it as an MP3 file on your computer. This software is extremely easy to use, so don't make it more complicated than it needs to be. Another alternative for Mac users is to check out Podcast Maker (www.potionfactory.com) where it does most of the work for you, then you publish to your podcast host.

If you're smart, you'll realize that you need to maximize your time for generating revenue, so instead of becoming an expert in podcast technology just use the software program automatically built into whatever podcasting host you choose. You will need to use such a hosting site, not unlike your website hosting company, because they will plug your podcast into what's called an RSS feed (really simple syndication). An RSS feed is simply how the folks who listen to you will receive your new podcasts. I recommend you choose a good host and create an account.

Here are some of the best podcast hosting sites. Unlike submitting articles, you only need to choose one to be your single host.

- www.jellycast.com
- www.podomatic.com
- www.itunes.com
- www.blogtalkradio.com
- www.hipcast.com
- www.libsyn.com
- www.podbean.com
- www.godaddy.com

Regardless of which route you choose, to improve the quality of your recording follow these tips:

- **Echoes:** When you record, do it in a room that is filled with lots of pictures, furniture, soft rugs, carpet, and so on. You could create a recording sound booth but you really do not need to do that. Lots of stuff in a room means lots less echo. Recording in a small barren room means echoes from hell.
- **Background noise:** Wherever you are going to record needs to be free from background noise so before you record just sit and listen for car noises, other people, trains, and so on. Turn off all phones, put all animals (and kids and spouses) out so they wont make any noise and don't crash things around yourself while you're recording (e.g., shuffling papers, clearing throat, banging chairs).
- **Dead space:** In any broadcast, dead space kills! Either be prepared as you make your recording, or if you get lost in the middle of it and find yourself with three seconds or more of silence, cut it out, save, and publish it.
- **Filler sucks:** By filler I mean the "um," "uh," "hmm," and any other noises you make when talking but are not sure what to say next. You may be surprised how many times you do this when you listen to your first recording. Try not to make filler noises when you're recording.
- **Body position:** Either sit upright or better yet stand when you make this recording because your body position can make a big difference in how energized you sound. Believe it or not, people can hear you slouch.

Once you finish your recording upload it to your podcast host site and you're good to go. Not only will others in the world be able to search for it, but you will want to take the link to that podcast and place it on your website. You can even link it to your blog on the same topic.

There is a wealth of information on podcasting on the Internet. Some of our consultants have created their own talk-radio show. To help build their authority they bring in guests and interview them on relevant topics that their target audience would care about.

Force Multiplier alert: Whenever you post any new podcast, be sure to share a link to it on your social media outlets, and make your RSS feed link easily visible on your website so visitors can register to receive all new feeds.

Workshop Marketing

If you're comfortable speaking in front of a crowd then consider using workshops as a marketing vehicle. If you are able to take your "article-lecture-presentation-video-podcast" material and build some activities around it, you could conduct a one- to three-hour workshop for attendees.

The only real downside to workshops is that it may be the first vehicle you have to actually put pants on for—since many of the previous marketing vehicles could have been done in your pajamas. Unlike the other marketing vehicles we've covered so far, this form is quite a bit more involved. You don't just get to write this one and publish it online somewhere. The length of your workshop, while up to you, is probably more in the one- to two-hour range, so you will need to add details, and build some interactive exercises or breakout activities.

One of the more important things to do is to figure out where you want to give this workshop, which brings up the question of whether you can conduct workshops online through virtual meeting technology. While it's possible to do this, I don't recommend it. The technology exists so that's not the problem, but one of the main benefits of this form of marketing is that it involves physically meeting prospects. Actually talking to and getting to know the participants afterwards is a big benefit to this vehicle if you ask me. If you want to make it virtual just turn it into a webinar. Keep workshops live.

Deciding where to hold workshops can be tricky. Finding an available room at a nearby hotel is never an issue, but that will run you some nice change depending on the city. Your Chamber of Commerce should be able to work with you for a free or very inexpensive room. If you're a member of any association or group where you can get a room for half a day for little to no money, that's a good option as well.

Be careful not to choose someplace that's free, but positions you badly. Using the local library or church hall screams, "I'm broke and this is the best I could afford." I'm not saying you need to spend thousands with a big buffet and fancy banners and handouts, but if you take the super cheap route you risk making the wrong impression.

The other decision you have to make is if you will do it for free or for a fee. This is a hotly debated topic. You can do your own research, but for me I've tried them both and here is my take:

- **For free:** Your objective is to get in front of potential clients and position yourself as an expert. If you can position it in conjunction with some group or association (e.g., Chamber, Rotary, etc.) then it's okay to conduct them for free because it's easier to position it as strictly continuing education inside an existing group. This group likely already conducts free education events, so you're just continuing in the same tradition. Free, in this case, is better as it will bring more attendees. Again, it will only bring in more attendees if in conjunction with some other organization or association.

- **For fee:** If you can't partner with another group, and are conducting your workshop in a hotel all alone, doing so for free backfires, in my opinion. It becomes pretty apparent to prospective attendees that you're the only one providing this workshop, in a hotel that everyone knows costs money, yet you're doing it for free? The impression is immediately, "There will be a firestorm of sales pitching happening." If you find yourself in this situation, then just place a moderate cost on the event (e.g., $79 to $279). This removes the concern (lessens it at least) that you will lock the doors and smother the attendees in sales goo. You should bear in mind that this is "workshop-*marketing*," not workshops as revenue tools. The latter is a legitimate way of making money, but different and not what I'm describing here, nor do these rules apply to that use of workshops. If you can't do it right just hold off on this vehicle until you can afford to. When you do squeeze the trigger on this approach, here are some additional tips to make sure you pull it off well:

- **Stick to the EBM model:** Remember to never deviate into a sales pitch. This format is no different from all the other marketing vehicles. Remember that this is marketing, not selling.

- **Follow the same format:** Stick to the "problem—cause—solution" format. The problem and cause will be covered more briefly, and the majority of the workshop will focus on the solution with practical, tangible takeaways.

- **Be Socratic:** Tell them up front what you're going to tell them (table of contents overview), then tell it to them (the body of your workshop), and at the end tell them what you told them (same table of contents slide). When you wrap it up at the end, offer to meet wherever and whenever necessary to continue to answer individual questions. This can lead to coffee afterwards, lunch the next day, or an office meeting next week. Leverage opportunities to move past the workshop because that's the entire reason you conducted it— to create one-on-one discussions with attendees to see if there's business to be had!

- **Keep it simple:** Use lots of bullet lists, lots of analogies, and lots of examples. Good workshops make complex topics easy to understand.

- **Keep it relevant:** Your objective should be to let each participant interact with activities and exercises where they can plug their own specific problems in.

- **Keep it interactive:** Group breakouts to answer questions, practicing techniques, and conducting mock exercises, are all great ways to stop talking and let the members work together. For every point you make, consider asking the audience for an example they've experienced. A good facilitator gets the group to talk as much or more than they do themselves.

- **Keep it moving:** It's easy to get lost down some bunny trail when one member asks lots of questions or is just not getting it. You must keep the flow going and respect the rest of the group so be prepared to recommend you continue a lengthy discussion offline after the workshop. Offline discussions, by the way, are your primary objective in workshop marketing, so embrace them wholeheartedly.

- **Shut up:** Unlike a lecturer, your role is that of facilitator. If you've been talking for more than 15 minutes, shut up and take questions, go to an activity that has participants talking, sharing, and working in breakout groups, and so on. Be attentive to any signs of questions, and ask, "Any questions?" frequently.

- **Make it visual:** Most people are visual learners. Make your presentation visually impactful, not 50 slides of boring bullets.

- **Make it coherent:** The best way to learn something is to see a clear and orderly process. Give the solution a name, give it steps, and give it some structure and order. Don't just provide five incoherent, unconnected things to do. Formalize those five things into your "Sales Development Process."

- **Laugh:** No big explanation here. Just have fun and enjoy it.
- **Use handouts:** The handouts are the one thing they will take with them, so print two slides per page from your presentation and include the original article you wrote at the end as well. Give the handouts a cover page with your company logo (always be branding) and contact info (business card).
- **Remember your objective:** You're conducting this workshop to generate leads. Don't end without giving them a call to action to talk more offline, talk more in-depth about their problem, and visit with them to explore their specific problem. A good way to achieve follow-up is offer to e-mail the presentation electronically, so you get their contact information. Either ask for a business card, or have a request form at their seat. Follow up with them after you send the presentation and probe what led them to attend the workshop.

Allan Miller, my Managing Director for Europe, has used workshop marketing as his primary vehicle for years and has leveraged it so effectively that he built a practice from start-up to seven figures in less than five years. Workshops are fantastic marketing vehicles, but only if you're very comfortable leading people through them. For him they've actually grown past just marketing to actual revenue generation on their own. If you're not comfortable facilitating groups of 20 to 30 people, you may never do a workshop and that's okay. The reason I give you 16 marketing vehicles is so you can pick the ones you're best at.

And, if you're okay with the concept of running one of these, but a little unsure as to how to do it, attend other workshops. If you liked a particular workshop, and it delivered value to you, then it was a good workshop. Learn what works for you and what doesn't, pattern your workshop accordingly and start fleshing out your own.

Book Marketing

There are some misconceptions about becoming an author and what it means to your success. There are two general areas of benefit to consider: financial and professional. From a professional standpoint, becoming a published author can definitely help to establish credibility and authority. On the financial side, however, writing a book isn't normally going to make you any real profits, let alone turn you into a millionaire. Let's break these two benefits down.

1. **Financial benefit:** Unless you're a perennial *New York Times* best-selling author (e.g., Tom Clancy or Stephen King), writing a book isn't going to make you independently wealthy. Where getting published *can* make a significant financial impact, though, is if you have your book connected to a platform. If your book is connected to some additional program you offer (e.g., consulting, coaching, or training), then it can definitely generate substantial revenue for you, but through sales in those areas alone. Just be clear that a book can be a big driver of profitability, but only as a marketing vehicle that helps you sell other programs, not as the end profit point itself.

2. **Professional benefit:** Using a book to build your credibility and make you an authority, on the other hand, is much more doable. Some people talk about a book as a great business card, and I would argue that this downplays its value quite a bit. A prospective client who sees that you've written a book will gain far more respect and see you as much more of an authority. Imagine being introduced at your next speaking engagement as "Author of ABC." How much more attractive will you be to those who want to partner with you to conduct workshops, trade groups, or associations interested in educational content, or your future clients? In this vein (i.e., as a positioning tool) being published can be a very big benefit.

Under Book Marketing, you also have two options:

1. **Traditional Publishing:** Being published through a traditional publishing company still holds the most prestige and while not 100 percent required making a bestseller list, it's damn near a 99.9 percent requirement. The channels and markets that determine bestseller status recognize very few self-published books. Getting it widely available on the shelves of brick and mortar bookstores is next to impossible as a self-published book.

    These companies bring a vast wealth of other benefits in the form of experience, manpower, design, editing, sales and marketing, distribution, etc. You will still be the one who drives roughly

90 percent of the book sales believe it or not, but the added value from a big publisher can make that a much easier task. The credibility and prestige a big publisher brings to your brand is very significant.

One of the biggest downsides to traditional publishing is their selectivity. They are inundated with new book submissions and typically only accept a fraction of one percent. Conservative estimates state approximately 3 out of every 10,000 books submitted get accepted (or 0.0003).

If you do decide on traditional publishing, you're best bet is to find a literary agent as that's the number one way to get noticed by a large publishing house. For a complete listing of literary agents in the United States, go to www.writers.net/agents.

2. **Self-publishing:** Nowadays there is no shortage of companies that will help you self-publish. Some try to get away from the self-published title by calling themselves vanity presses or boutique publishers, but they're self-publishing outlets. You can easily define a self-publishing company from a traditional publishing company through one irrefutable characteristic. No traditional publisher will ask you to pay them, and all self-publishers will. Prices for such companies range anywhere from $3,000 on the low end to $10,000, but I've even seen some that will sell you a bestselling book campaign for $300,000.

Not that there is anything wrong with self-publishing. If you aren't looking for worldwide distribution or if you're primary objective is to have a book to hand to clients or use in lectures as giveaways or for back of room sales, this is a great solution. If you can afford to spend money up front, self-publishing can keep you owning 90 percent of the royalties. If you're just getting started, self-publishing may be a great alternative to traditional publishing.

There is a wealth of information you would still need to actually self-publish a book so research online for that topic and consider the various options available to you.

The key to using a book as a marketing tool is to ask yourself what your objective is. Why do you want to write a book? It takes an enormous amount of time and energy to create a book, so know up front why you're doing it, and make sure you select the option that is right for those reasons.

There are some universal steps you can take to use that book as a marketing vehicle. In short, use it as new content for the rest of your marketing vehicles, as described in the following nine activities.

1. **Break it apart:** Repurpose the content of your book by turning one item into 100 items. Make as many stand-alone articles as you can out of the book and generate blogs, articles, videos, and so on. Turn it into an audiobook and an e-book, and sell those on your website too.

2. **Speak on it:** There's nothing easier to speak on than a book you wrote. Create a speech around the core concepts of the book, but make sure it's education-based. You must select one or two core concepts that you can deliver 100 percent in that speech. It's fine to not be able to get into the whole book as you can sell the rest of the story to attendees. As a published author your speaking fees should rise dramatically, by the way.

3. **Build a workshop around it:** Craft a half-day or full-day workshop around the book and its solutions.

4. **Videos and podcasts:** Plug the content of your book into other marketing vehicles like videos and podcasts.

5. **Website:** Make a stand-alone page on your website where people can read excerpts, see testimonials, and purchase the book. You may want to buy a unique URL for this page that ties into the title of your book.

6. **Tease it:** Offer one or two complete chapters (the juiciest and most powerful) on your website for free download, but only once someone registers. Ask them for their name and e-mail address and you will e-mail them a link to download those chapters instantly. This is a good way of building your e-mail list, which you will market all of your other offerings to (e.g., blog, articles, speeches, videos, etc.). So even if you don't sell the book, you've used it to grow your marketing pool.

7. **Bulk sales:** Approach trade groups and associations about partnering with them to promote your book as a great value addition to their members. You *will* need to make it financially attractive to them. Negotiate a revenue split, get them to push the hell out of it to their database, and offer a free educational webinar, series, or lecture to go along with it. Find an association that moves 3,000

copies and you could earn $15,000 in cash while really marketing your larger offerings or platform.

8. **Leverage it:** Remember, no book is really only a means to an end. Wherever or however you use it, make sure you leverage it as a tool to drive prospective clients to your more substantial offerings!

9. **Having a platform:** The main reason you want to author a book is to drive sales to your platform and build credibility. A "platform" simply means a system that accommodates the various programs you offer. Your book's greatest financial benefit will be to attract prospects to your platform (e.g., website, webinars, conferences, etc.) where you sell solutions (e.g., workshops, training, coaching, etc.). Getting a book out there won't do your business any financial good if you don't have something bigger to offer those who read it.

If you're planning on writing a book then make sure you have a platform to draw readers into. Write in your book about a specific process you champion (your coaching methodology, let's say), or introduce them to your "five-step leadership development process" and teach them what it's all about in the book itself. But, you *must* then connect that book with a website where readers can go learn more about that process, watch educational videos on it, find an offer from you to interact live, and eventually become paying customers.

Before you start writing word one of your new book, check out Amazon.com to see what books already exist in your areas of specialization and see if there's some glaring hole that is just crying to be filled. If there is, give it some consideration, and then give it a try.

Drip or E-Mail Marketing

Drip marketing, sometimes called *autoresponder campaigns* or *life cycle e-mail marketing*, involves automatically sending a series of e-mails to a prospective client over a set period of time. The reason you should be most interested in it is the "automated" part.

I've already mentioned the old adage in marketing of having to touch someone seven times before getting noticed. Drip campaigns are a modern day application of this concept. Instead of mailing a series of flyers, or repeating a series of TV commercials, many marketers today employ a drip campaign to achieve this level of penetration. Some do it very poorly and are what you would know as "spam." However, if done correctly, and with permission, it is a very effective way of developing a relationship remotely that turns into a real business relationship. The big difference is that you will not use an e-mail campaign to sell anything directly. That is what turns a drip-campaign into spam. Like all the other vehicles, this is education-based marketing, not selling.

In my world, a drip campaign is an automated e-mail program that sends out small educational e-mails concerning one specific topic, which starts after a prospect registers to watch one of my EBM videos, or downloads an EBM article, or any other marketing vehicle I choose.

If you remember back when I talked about setting up your website, I said you needed to tell your web developer that you would need some auto-responder software because you were going to create a lead-generating website instead of just another brochure site. It is by using a drip campaign that you achieve that lead generation. Here's how it works:

- You post an EBM article on your website and make it available for download.
- Your web developer has set up an autoresponder program (my two favorites are: InfusionSoft or AWeber). These have a minor monthly cost, but it's well worth it.
- On your website, there is a box where any visitor can request that EBM article. In Internet marketing this is called a "squeeze box." This box is plugged into your autoresponder software. Its sole purpose is to allow any visitor to enter their name and e-mail address, and be approved to either download the article or receive it in an e-mail.
- The main reason you want to do this is to build a database of leads. The autoresponder software captures their contact info, and sends them an e-mail asking for authorization to send them that article. This is important so you don't run afoul of anti-spam laws by sending e-mails to someone who hasn't "opted-in" to receive them first.
- The visitor enters their information and receives the valuable document (or video, podcast, etc.) they wanted.

■ Here's where it gets interesting. Once they receive that document, your autoresponder campaign begins to send them e-mails that you've prewritten, over some predefined period of time or frequency, that seek to educate them more on whatever you gave them. It is this "dripping" of small helpful e-mails that helps create a relationship.

That's the principle. To do it correctly, ethically, and efficaciously, however, there are certain rules you must follow:

■ Any e-mail you send must be educational in nature and concerning the thing they received from you (e.g., drip e-mails that help explain key points in the article on leadership).
■ These e-mails are *not* sales e-mails! Follow the EBM guidelines you've already learned.
■ Each e-mail should include contact information and a call to action to reach out to you if they have any problems or questions regarding the content of the document in question.
■ All drip campaigns come to an end with a definitive call to action.

Here's a real-life example from my own consulting practice:

■ I write an article on the keys to effective leadership. In that article I described some key characteristics of effective leaders and some steps a company could take to hire more effective leaders in the future.
■ I place the title and some choice excerpts from it on my website for anyone to review.
■ Using autoresponder software, my web developer created a box that asks for an e-mail address from anyone interested in reading the full article, so we can send it to them. I've done this with videos, profiles, and e-books, too.
■ Once someone receives that article, my drip campaign immediately sends them another e-mail thanking them for their interest, telling them that they should have received the article by now, and giving them my contact info if they did not receive it. At the end of that very short "thank you" e-mail I let them know I will be sending them some more e-mails to expand on each of the

core concepts in that article (i.e., even more education on this topic).

■ The next day they receive an e-mail with "Tip #1 to effectively hiring leaders," where I give them just one small paragraph of pure educational content. At the end of that e-mail I also give them my contact info and offer to answer any questions they have.

■ Two days later they receive another e-mail from me with tip #2. This process automatically repeats over the course of eight e-mails, with eight tips, spread out over perhaps two weeks. Through the autoresponder software, anyone who no longer desires to receive these educational e-mails can simply click a button and they opt out.

■ Each e-mail has the same boilerplate contact info and call to action to call me if they have any specific questions.

■ The last two e-mails give more education on the topic, but then invite them to attend a webinar on that same topic. Usually a good number of people attend those webinars. I generate several paying clients each time and life is good.

The key to the effectiveness of this approach is that in the beginning when you set your campaign up, you write all your education e-mails at one time. They are then loaded into the software and it does the rest of the work from there. Your website could be sending an article, and then educational support e-mails to someone five time zones away at three in the morning while you sleep. The importance is that you've automated this marketing program so you are free to focus on other marketing or revenue generating activities.

I like to think of a drip campaign as "drip coaching." The visitor to my site received something of great value, and at no additional charge they received a series of coaching e-mails from me that helped create a relationship where one didn't exist before, position myself as an authority, and provide some calls to action to interact.

Remember how I wrote some chapters back that you can't control whether the prospect is ready to buy or not, but you have to make sure you're there when they decide they are? This is the same principle that drives a good drip campaign. It won't ever be designed to sell consulting, but it effectively attracts prospects into one-on-one discussions with you where you can then convert them into paying clients. Statistically, future clients are 10 times more likely to reach out to someone who they have a relationship with when they need help. Interestingly enough, psychologically that relationship can be perceived to exist even if the prospect has only read something you wrote.

Autoresponders can get much more complicated than this simple function. Once you master the basic level, talk with your web developer about more complex campaigns later. These programs are huge time savers, and can work wonders to build your network but only when you respect your recipients properly.

Referral Marketing

Referrals are absolutely a marketing vehicle. The problem is that many consultants don't treat them as such. They're so effective because of the nature of what you sell and whom you sell it to. Like other professionals, business consulting is not something that you can effectively market through advertising or other typical marketing vehicles.

When was the last time you dialed a financial planner after seeing his face plastered on the back of a city bus? Conversely, ask yourself how you found those authorities you do work with. More than likely you found them through a referral from someone you trust. The social proof of an endorsement from someone you already know and trust is the most powerful means of growth for our profession. Some experts have measured that almost 85 percent of all new business in consulting comes through referrals.

And that's why this section is so very important. Having a strong referral program will be absolutely vital to your growth! Now, when I say strong referral program let me start with what is *not* a strong program:

- Infrequently asking friends and family to refer you—is not.
- Giving existing clients extra business cards and hoping they will refer you to someone—is not.
- Even actually asking your client for a name, then following up directly with them yourself—is not.

A strong referral program, however, has three characteristics:

1. Is formal. It is built into your actual deliverable to the client, not infrequently or casually asked for.

2. Asks the client to actually make the introduction themselves, not hand you a name.
3. Represents a hard financial value to the referring client.

Let's dig deeper into each one of these three to see what you have to do to create a strong and effective referral program:

1. **It is formal.** That means you can't just make a passing comment, or ask, "Would you mind making a referral to anyone you know who might need my help?" If you treat it informally, it implies it's not terribly important; thus it is deemed so by your client as well. Make it formal by literally putting it in writing. In your actual contract you need to add a section at the end that states, "Referral Program" and write out for the client that, as part of this contract, you will expect two strong referrals from them at the time of their choosing and assuming they are satisfied with your work. Here's what I put in my contracts. *"As a business consultant referrals are a vital part of my business. As long as you are satisfied with the results of my work, and at a time of your choosing, I would ask that you commit to make a minimum of two referrals to people you know who you believe could benefit from my services. In return, I agree to reduce the cost of my proposal by 10 percent in appreciation for this valuable service."*

   This request is 100 percent optional, and if the client isn't interested, you don't have to take 10 percent off. I've found that most people sincerely have an interest in helping others. Also, notice how I use the word "commit" as it carries the significance of meaning "I intend," not just "agree to" or "will consider."

2. **Ask the client to make the referral for you.** Many consultants just ask for the names of someone that their client thinks might be interested in hearing from them. While this is an acceptable fallback tactic if must be, the more ideal approach is to ask that they themselves tell the referral about you and give them your information. In this way, the prospect hears it from the client's mouth and the social proof is significantly greater than if you were to cold-call them. However, you will ask your client to give you the contact info of the referral as well, and you will indeed follow up with them yourself afterwards. Now, when you reach out to that referral you're doing two

things. First you're keeping a promise to your client (e.g., "Johnny Client said he thought we should talk about X, Y, and Z and I promised him I would follow up with you." By doing this you're fulfilling a promise made to your client, so use the word "promise" in whatever introduction you think best. Second, when the prospect hears your name, you're not a cold introduction. He should recognize you and associate you with the social proof and testimony he received from someone he already trusts.

Side note: one of the reasons this approach is so effective is that it returns somewhat qualified prospects. If I were to just ask my client for two names and phone numbers, he could easily return two leads that are in his contact database, but have absolutely no problems worth talking about right now.

3. **Give it a monetary value.** I give this request a true monetary value for the client. It's only fair that if you're asking them to do something that is valuable to you, you offer to share that value with them. If they aren't comfortable with agreeing to this, there is zero pressure from me. I move on without even considering negotiating this term with them. If they say "No," then done deal. As for 10 percent, that's totally up to you but offer them some tangible benefit as a sign of its value to you.

Effective Partnership Marketing

Somewhat related to referral-based marketing, partnership marketing is different and more of a quid-pro-quo. This is the practice of creating strategic relationships with other professionals who are neither your client, nor competition, to refer business to each other. Examples of such could include: corporate attorneys, accountants, bankers, or IT professionals.

In short, as you're out there networking keep an eye out for any other professionals you find who cater to the same audience. When you find them suggest the possibility of working together to refer potential clients to each other. When you do this, though, make sure you start with their benefit by letting them know that from time to time you come across business clients who could use their help and you'd like to know you could refer them over. Do not approach the discussion seeking a referral from them first.

And there is no monetary compensation for these referrals. This is not a commission-based marketing program. These are 100 percent free referrals and the only string attached is that they agree to return the favor the next time they come across a client who could use some consulting help.

Make sure to provide them with a complete listing of all the services you provide, so they know what to be looking for. When you do this, don't hand them a list of your solution names or even what services you provide, rather give them a list of all the niche markets you target and the specific problems you help these businesses solve.

The list of potential partners doesn't have to be bankers and attorneys. Consider Chamber of Commerce employees, financial planners, website developers, graphic designers, and so on. Basically, anyone you meet who provides professional services to the exact same market you do could become a strategic partner in this vehicle.

This means you should consider other independent consultants too. Instead of seeing them as competition, consider finding other consultants who specialize in areas where you don't, because not only might you need to invite them in to provide services you don't, but vice versa. Whether you follow the "keep your enemies even closer" mentality, or are open to partnering, getting to know lots of other consultants is always a good move.

To work, however, this model needs to be fed. If they make referrals to you, but you never reciprocate, they will eventually stop making them. This model requires a balance and mutual benefit.

Network-Based Marketing (i.e., Networking)

Business consulting is a people business. It is face-to-face, social, interactive, and very much about the ability to charm people. If you're someone for whom the thought of mingling amid 100 other business people is disconcerting, than you will likely have a hard go of effectively networking and building a profitable practice. If you can't develop a human network, it will be very hard to survive as an independent management consultant.

When it comes to the topic of networking effectively, since I'm only covering the basics here, I strongly recommend reading anything by Dr. Ivan Misner, who I consider to be one of the world's authorities on the subject. Specifically, I recommend *The 29% Solution*. That said, let's cover the foundation of effective networking.

The biggest mistake anyone can make is to view networking as selling. It's not! Showing up at a networking event with the intent of selling anything means you might as well not get out of your car. Networking is aptly named, as it is just that—creating a network of contacts. Networking events are not intended to be instant referral opportunities. They didn't name it "sell-working" for a reason.

When you network bear these rules in mind:

- **Select the right group.** Pick networking functions or groups that either hold the promise to be filled with your target audience, or other professionals you could partner with for referrals.
- **Follow the EBM mentality.** Seek to give and get to know others and build a relationship, not take away business.
- **Bring lots of business cards.** This speaks for itself.
- **Bring your Unique Value Proposition.** Dust off the Unique Value Proposition you created earlier, and have it warmed up and ready to go when someone asks you what you do.
- **Think like a date.** If you act like you're on a first date, you should know that your goal is to talk more about the other person than yourself. Everyone hates it when they get stuck in a conversation where the other person can't stop talking about themselves. The subject of the discussion should revolve around the other person much more than it does you.
- **Come early—stay late.** A lot of good networking actually happens when it's less crowded before and after the actual event.
- **Note the card.** Make notes on the back of cards to remind yourself of specifics. Trust me, you'll forget important notes after meeting lots of people.
- **Be moderately prolific.** You don't want to attend too few, or too many, networking events. One a month is too little; however, 5 to 10 a week is too many. While it is an effective part of growing your practice, it isn't the only part. Shoot for two to three a week in the beginning until you build a strong list of contacts, then slow down to about two to three a month.
- **Respect the contact.** Some consultants make the big mistake of abusing the business card in their hand. They add the person to

their e-mail list without asking, then smother them with e-mails or marketing brochures. I think the most effective way to build that relationship is to get that new contact added to your list, but you must ask them if that's okay first! The best way I've found to do that is send an initial "nice to meet you" e-mail and ask if it would be okay to add them to your "executive education" series. Don't ask, "Can I add you to my newsletter list?" Don't ask, "Can I put you on my e-mail list?" Make it specific, about executive education and give one juicy example (e.g., Leadership Development Article).

■ **Make a great second impression.** I'm a big fan of mailing a handwritten "nice to meet you" note on actual card stock. It's good to e-mail, as it's easier for the person to put you into their contact list, but mailing a physical note as well, with another business card inside, is not only different, it's memorable.

The second biggest mistake consultants make is to only network when they are out of work and are looking for more business. Networking is an ongoing activity. It doesn't deliver clients overnight so building and maintaining a network is something that has to be nurtured long-term. Even when your calendar is fat with paying client work, you must keep your network fresh and growing.

The following list shows you where to find networking opportunities. This should never be a problem for you as even small towns have networking opportunities to take advantage of. Your local Chamber of Commerce should have a bunch, plus lists of others. Check out your local BNI network (the professional networking group founded by Dr. Misner). You can check out the following websites as well:

Facebook (www.facebook.com)   Net Party (www.netparty.com)
LinkedIn (www.linkedin.com)   Twtvite (www.twtvite.com)
Meetup (www.meetup.com)   When (www.when.com)
Eventbrite (www.eventbrite.com)   Yelp (www.yelp.com)

Just remember that networking is a long-term play. It takes time to develop these relationships so start early (even before your doors are officially open), and don't ever stop. People buy from people they know. Get to know a lot of people!

Research-Based Marketing

One of my favorite means of marketing is a take on education-based marketing. I call it "research-based marketing." It's definitely not for everyone, but in my opinion this approach is a triple win scenario. Here's why:

- Win #1: It removes defensive roadblocks.
- Win #2: It creates a demand.
- Win #3: It positions you as the authority and thought leader.

So what exactly is research-based marketing? I coined the term to describe the process of conducting research for marketing purposes. In this concept you would approach prospective clients with a request to join you in a research study you are conducting into a significant problem in their industry. Here's a real-world example:

Johnny Consultant specializes in sales development. Johnny decides to conduct a research-based marketing campaign. He settles on researching what differentiates a great salesperson from the rest. Not being a scientist, Johnny identifies a professor of business from the nearby university and approaches her about working with him on this project. Since Johnny has used diagnostic profiles that measure sales traits, the hypothesis becomes, "The best performing salespeople possess certain measureable traits or characteristics that poor salespeople do not." With her help, the two work out some specifics for the study and Johnny sets about contacting the 10 largest sales companies in his target market.

Given that he is approaching them about getting their help in a groundbreaking research study (in association with a reputable university), rather than trying to sell them something, the majority of the companies he approaches jump on board. Johnny coordinates with each company in the study to have all of their salespeople complete the 10-minute online sales profile, and he ranks their sales forces based purely on sales results against quota.

With data in hand, the professor sets to work crunching numbers and in short order comes out with a set of traits that only correlate with the top performers. Together Johnny and the professor write up a short white paper on their little study and Johnny mails it to the CEOs and Directors of Sales in all the companies that took part in the study. He also follows up with each separately and goes over the results.

Seeing that the research has identified seven core attributes that only the top performers possessed, the companies ask Johnny how well their own sales staff compares to the findings of the study. They also want to know how they can develop those salespeople who don't possess those traits, and they are interested in being able to identify these traits in all new hiring candidates. And thus we find Johnny in negotiations with several new prospects for training and hiring solutions.

Never the slacker, Johnny gets in touch with associations in that industry, and shares his findings with them, asking if they would be interested in having him present these findings at their next convention. They are; he does; and soon Johnny is presenting proposals to help many other companies identify and develop these traits as well.

See how easy that is? I'm smiling as I write this, as I know it may seem like a daunting objective up front. In reality, though, it doesn't have to be that hard. If you're smart and decide to work with a researcher from a local university or college, they will know everything about the scientific method needed, so no worries. This leaves you to be the one who reaches out to potential participant companies, helps to present the findings, and sells the consulting engagements designed to fix the problem.

To utilize a research-based marketing approach, follow these eight steps:

1. **Identify a target audience.** Likely this is the primary audience you are already focused on. In addition to approaching several independent companies, consider approaching an association who would love the added credibility and value for their members, and who could easily get several of their best member organizations to join the study.
2. **Identify their greatest pain/problem.** You should already know this.

3. **Draft a very simple proposal.** By "simple" I literally mean write out in a standard Word document the following:
   a. **Formulate the question.** Statement about #1 and #2 above, but write it in the form of a question (e.g., Why do some salespeople succeed where others fail? What is it that explains the difference?).
   b. **Create a Hypothesis.** A hypothesis is an educated guess or proposition that explains why an observation or fact exists. In our example above, Johnny's hypothesis could be, "Certain natural traits or characteristics exist that support one's ability to sell. Those salespeople who possess these traits outperform those who do not." You're the expert. Why do you think the problem exists? Working with your professorial partner, draft a hypothesis. Your hypothesis should also be refutable, which simply means it is something that can be *proven* false. Stating the hypothesis, "The best salespeople are those who had better childhoods" wouldn't be a very good hypothesis as "good" is subjective.
   c. **Make a prediction.** State what you think the outcome of your research will be (e.g., "Of the 25 traits we can measure, we expect to find at least five that correlate positively with performance.").
4. **Select your diagnostic tool.** Determine which profile you want to use and give this instrument to all of the salespeople. There are tons of valid personality profiles on the market today. In Chapter 8 I will give you a list of the top profile companies, so you can decide for yourself. These can be simple tools that don't require significant training in order to use effectively, and all are automated and online.
5. **Measure (test).** Have all the salespeople complete the profile, and aggregate the scores into a single Excel spreadsheet. Special note: make sure you have a large enough population to study. General rule of thumb is to have 10 participants for every one item being studied at a minimum. If you use a profile that measures 20 sales traits, you should have a minimum of 200 salespeople in the study. This is why you approach multiple companies in the same industry selling the same product or service.
6. **Crunch the data (analyze).** Let your academic partner crunch the data and see what she finds to correlate with performance. Sorry for

the highfalutin words, but typically the statistical partner will conduct some form of regression analysis seeking to understand the relationship between the dependent and independent variables. In short, ask them which measurable traits or qualities seem to be connected only with superior sales results.

7. **Share your findings.** Write up a white paper, and start marketing it to all the companies you can. At this point you go back through this list of marketing vehicles and select the ones you think will work best to spread the word. Write about it, speak about it, and make presentations and movies and podcasts about it.

8. **Build a platform around it.** This is the most important part of this whole process! Since you're not trying to become a tenured professor, and you don't get paid to conduct and publish research (the likely reward for the professor you work with, by the way, plus a little sales commission, is a good idea as well), your reward for doing all of this work is to catapult yourself onto the scene in that industry, speaking on the findings and talking with companies about how you could help them identify these traits in their own salespeople (and develop them or improve hiring if necessary).

If you follow the logic of this model I hope you see how powerful it can be in positioning you as an authority, and creating demand for your services. It's an ultimate authority builder and lead generator! Granted it's not for everyone, but before you dismiss it as something only a PhD should consider, know that I don't have a PhD, nor do any of the hundreds of other consultants I know who've done something very similar with great success.

Press Release Marketing

One great way to get free publicity is through press release marketing. This is a strategy that you can manage all on your own, you shouldn't have to spend any money to do it, and you don't need to hire some expensive PR firm. All you will do is craft a killer press release, share it through a whole lot of vehicles, and give reporters something that helps them do their job. If you help reporters do their job, they will help you do yours.

The first thing you need to know is that the headline and sub-header of your press release will either catapult your release into an editor's hands, or crush your release into a tiny ball that finds itself soaring through the air towards a round can.

Here are the general guidelines for writing a killer press release:

1. **Think like the reporter!!!** For our purposes here, my use of "reporter" is interchangeable with editors, producers, writers, TV hosts, radio hosts, and so on. Not only is this the first step in effectively using press releases for marketing, but also it warrants triple exclamation points because it's that damn important. Fail to do this and don't bother with any other steps to follow because you will just be wasting your time. To achieve this empathetic point of view, you must realize that reporters don't give a crap about your business. Start by realizing that the person reading your press release cares only about anything that helps them achieve their objectives, which is to write a story that is compelling and interesting to their readers. Stories that flatter you, market your business, or serve your needs only, will never see the light of day. Don't ask yourself, "How can I get them to help promote my business?" Ask, "How can I help make their job easier?" Also, thinking from a reporter's perspective means never using "I" or "we" unless you're quoting someone else.
   a. What reporters don't care about:
      i. You
      ii. Your product
      iii. Your company
      iv. Your success
   b. What reporters do care about:
      i. Their readers' interests.
      ii. Their objective to write what those readers want to hear.
      iii. Your ability to give them an interesting story (which means a story of interest to their readers, not an interesting story about you).
2. **Develop a killer angle.** Developing a killer angle means crafting a story (which is what a press release really is—a very short story) that is compelling to the reader, not you. Killer angles are:
   a. **Unique/different.** Your opening yet another consulting firm is definitely not unique or very different. You being the first in the

industry to solve problem X, or taking the contrarian view everyone else says is wrong, is interesting. This is where you really need to think outside the box and find something to talk about that isn't the same old thing yet again. The plumbing company that includes "We make house calls" in their marketing is far from unique.

b. **Tangible.** You spouting off about some theory isn't tangible. You informing readers how to improve real-world results is much better. Processes and techniques aren't tangible. The results they return, though, are tangible. Your press release must show the reporter what problem exists, what causes it, and how it can be resolved. Ending your story with "And my company helps these companies solve it" ain't gonna cut it. You must give them the actual solution.

c. **Beneficial to large audiences.** Your describing how to solve a problem suffered by the 100 experts in rain forest fungi may be very beneficial to those 100, but your describing how to solve a problem suffered by anyone who manages more than two people is more what you're shooting for. Avoid "insiders" discussions in your press releases and target larger audiences.

d. **Absent of fluff.** Words are valuable in press releases. Think like a Twitter user here. Wasting any words on describing: "great service," "reliable," "low priced," or any other hyperbole is not only wasting valuable space, but turning you into a salesperson, which reporters hate. And steer clear of overblown fluff like "revolutionary," "groundbreaking," "amazing," or similarly puffed up descriptors.

e. **Edgy or Shocking.** While you can't always do this, have fun with your press release. Remember that the reporter reading it has already read countless others that day. Make them laugh, shock them, or even say something that might upset someone else, and you will grab their attention. Of course you need to be professional and not offensive, and never lie! Writing about "Revelations in improving sales training" is anything but edgy. Writing on "Why most sales training sucks" is a totally different beast. "What the best companies do" maxes out the yawn factor, yet "Where stupid leaders come from" will at least get a first read.

3. **Craft an awesome header.** The objective of your title or header is to hook the reporter reading it. Leave your ego at home. You've got just a few precious words to catch their attention.
    a. Example of a crappy header: "New consulting practice opens in Yawn Harbor township."
    b. Example of an awesome header: "Local consulting firm explains why so many are out of work," or "Local manufacturing company makes a miraculous comeback" (due to your help, of course).

4. **Craft an equally awesome subheader.** The subheader is your opportunity to share more great information and connect the story even more. Think of the header and subheader as the one-two punch in boxing. The header grabs their attention, while the subheader closes the deal and sets the hook.
    a. Example of crappy subheader: "ABC Consulting is now offering an entire series of educational seminars on best practices in leadership."
    b. Example of a great subheader: "Local consultant helps local manufacturing do what they said was impossible, and saves 500 jobs."

5. **Write a stand-alone lead.** In journalism, the lead means the lead paragraph. It is here that you must include the who, what, why, when, where, and how of your story. Write this paragraph assuming the reader will never go any further. You need to give them everything they would need to get a story rolling, or permission from their editor to research it at least, in this one paragraph. The lead is a cold, factual, almost technical description of the story. Follow Seargent Friday's motto and stick to "Just the Facts" (apologies to our younger readers for the *Dragnet* reference).

6. **In the body.** The body of the press release shouldn't be much of a body (think Kate Moss stranded at sea). There's no burden to fill an entire page. Short is good, but only if it's complete. If you need to support your argument further, or provide more evidence, the body is the place to do that. Quotes are a great resource for the body of the release as well (e.g., "Sales have increased 93 percent," said company President John Smiley). Ask your clients to provide a quote that backs up your header and subheader, not directly pitches your company.

7. **Wrap it all up with a boilerplate.** The final paragraph of a press release is called the boilerplate. Boiler manufacturers in the last

century used to stamp a plate with their name on it to show everyone who made that boiler. Later, companies would produce their own metal printing plate with their company information on it and give it to the printers, so if they wrote a story about that company they could use those preprepared plates and save time and money. In effect your boilerplate is nothing more than an "About Us" tag at the bottom of every press release. Here are some tips to leverage your boilerplate:

a. **Keep it short.** Don't make it longer than four or five sentences max.
b. **List company headquarters.** This is important for journalists interested in local stories.
c. **Founding date.** If you're brand new, you may want to avoid this one.
d. **Type.** Are you a private or publicly traded company?
e. **What is your Unique Value Proposition?** You should already have your Unique Value Proposition ready to go.
f. **Who is your target audience?** Who do you help?
g. **Geography.** Do you only work with local clients, regional, national, or international even?
h. **Once you're done.** At the very end, I like the old-school practice of placing three # symbols, and then providing your contact info. Social media and website links are good here as well.

Here's a sample of boilerplate from my own company:

Innermetrix Inc. is a privately held corporation headquartered in Philadelphia PA USA, with offices in Europe, the Middle East, Asia and South Africa. Since its inception in 1998, we have helped over 1,750 independent management consultants in over 23 countries establish and grow profitable consulting practices with our unique products and services.

To speak with Jay Niblick about this story, please contact him at jay@email.com, (800) 123-4567 and visit www.innermetrix.com for more information.

8. **Make everything relevant and current.** Another vital aspect of your press release is that it must be relevant and current. Don't just write a killer angle, then leave it hanging in the air. Read the news and figure out how your story connects to something extremely

relevant in the press today. This is actually quite easy because the market you are speaking to (that's the reporter) is telling you what to write about every single day. The news industry spends billions figuring out what is relevant and hot, and they tell you instantly by posting it in the news. Leverage their billion-dollar investment, and simply spin your news in the exact same areas. For example, if all the news can talk about is how horrible the economy is, instead of talking about leadership development, talk about how effective leadership is the key differentiator among companies that are surviving today's horrible economy. If all the news can talk about is politics, talk about how small businesses (your true target audience) will be affected by the candidates.

9. **Communicate with them in a way they will appreciate:** There is accepted etiquette in dealing with reporters. Make sure you respect the following:

   a. **Be sure you do everything above first!** Before you reach out to the first editor, ensure you've covered all of the tips above. Then send your release.

   b. **Don't call them to see if they received your release.** These people are absolutely inundated with releases. The last thing they need is you feeling special and bothering them with a phone call or voicemail to see if they received it. It's implied that if they got it, and they liked it, they will follow up with you.

   c. **When you do call, respect their deadlines.** It's okay to call if you have questions about how to submit, or when, and so on. If you do, though, make sure you aren't bothering them in the middle of a deadline crunch. Most stories are submitted in the morning, which means the journalist is working on the next day's stories from about 2:00 PM local time and for the rest of their day. The best time to attempt a call is between 9:00 AM and 12:00 PM at the latest.

   d. **Don't overwhelm them.** The hallmark sign of a horrible salesperson is that they "show up and throw up," as we used to say in sales. This simply means showing up and regurgitating a nonstop sales pitch. If you do end up on the phone with someone, don't dive head first into some scripted pitch explaining everything your release already said. Ask your question, thank them, and get off the line.

e. **Leverage technology.** Everyone has voicemail nowadays, and there's nothing at all wrong with using it. The reporter is a very busy person. They will appreciate getting the message without having to actually speak to you (no offense). If you get their voicemail, leave a *short* message regarding who you are, why you are calling, the title of your release, and phone number.

Where to Take Your Awesome Press Release

Once you've written the world's most kick-ass press release, share it with as many outlets as possible. Below is a list of some of the top places to submit your press release. Every single one of them is completely free, but some do require you to take a few minutes to register an account. Pick several, or picking them all would be a really good idea. In this exercise I'm a big fan of more being more. Here's my top 25.

1. www.Expertclick.com
2. www.clickpress.com
3. www.prnewswire.com
4. www.npr.org
5. www.directionsmag.com
6. www.prlog.org
7. www.newswiretoday.com
8. www.pr-inside.com
9. www.24-7pressrelease.com
10. www.pr.com
11. www.prleap.com
12. www.free-press-release.com
13. www.pressbox.co.uk
14. www.onlineprnews.com
15. www.przoom.com
16. www.openpr.com
17. www.1888pressrelease.com
18. www.theopenpress.com
19. www.free-press-release-center.info
20. www.ukprwire.com
21. www.pressexposure.com
22. www.mediasyndicate.com

23. www.seenation.com
24. www.addpr.com
25. www.pressreleasecirculation.com

Always be on the lookout for new press release opportunities in conjunction with any new services you add (couched in the terms of the benefits to the reporter, of course), new positive results or case studies, or new media attention in an area previously worked in by you, but not a hot topic for them.

Nonstarters in Marketing

There are a few forms of marketing that I simply can't recommend. You will find those out there right now extolling the virtues of some of these, but I haven't seen any of them work worth a damn so I figured I would save you some time. Since they're no good, I won't take too much of your valuable time telling you why, but I think it's important to make at least a short case against each.

Here's just the quick review of why you should avoid each of these as time-wasters or zero-return items:

- **Newsletters.** They are old, passé, require a lot of time to build properly, and you and every other person on the planet has one. If you ever want to scream "I'm just like everyone else," just mention that you have a newsletter.
- **Paid advertising.** When your practice reaches seven figures you can revisit this one. While it can be very effective in certain industries, or in widely distributed publications, the cost-to-reward ratio is just impossible for the new or fledgling consultant. Revisit once you're cruising down profitability pike.
- **Pay-per-click advertising (PPC).** This is paying someone like Google Adwords a small fee every time someone on the Internet clicks on your link. Most people realize that the top search results are paid for, and avoid them. Don't get me wrong. They can be very effective, but what you need to spend to actually show up there, you most likely can't afford. And what you can afford won't get you crap for placement. Plus, you're not paying for customers, just eyeballs on your website, which is a whole different story.

- **Direct mail.** Even the direct mail association itself reports that response rates have dropped to an all-time low of 0.5 percent. I can think of a whole lot of other things I'd rather try than something that returns one-half of 1 percent.
- **Cold calling.** No justification needed. If by this point in the book you still think that making cold calls as a professional consultant will position you and your work properly, I've lost.
- **Telemarketing.** Knowing that cold calling is the worst marketing mistake you could ever make, why would someone think it was okay to spend precious money to pay someone else to do it for you?
- **Flyers.** Really? If you are a consultant who specializes in helping pizza parlors, cover bands, and yoga instructors, then perhaps marketing flyers will work. Otherwise, I'm not even going there.

These are your 16 marketing vehicles. Take them on a test drive, get to know them, and decide which ones are the best fit for you. I recommend you practice one at a time, though. Don't overwhelm yourself by attempting to pull off a bunch of these at once, at least not the first time. You don't have to use all of them by any means. Just know that the more of them you use the greater your profits will be! Once you've used them once, you're safe to start using several all at the same time.

Now that we've completely covered marketing, let's move to the last stage in the entire process—sales.

7

Why Selling Sucks—The Profits from Your Practice

IN BOTH 2010 AND 2011 my company, Innermetrix, conducted polls of over 6,000 independent consultants. This survey was designed to help us understand how satisfied the general consulting community was with the results of their sales efforts. The results of that survey highlighted a critical issue.

While 99 percent of the respondents felt that "getting more business" was their most critical issue, 98 percent felt an equally strong dislike for the act of selling. Now that's what I would call a bit of a dilemma.

The problem: Independent consultants need to sell—but they hate to sell.

With such a significant problem, it is tempting to jump immediately to the solution of how to fix it. Before you can fix a problem, though, you have to understand its cause. Otherwise you are treating the symptoms.

Below are the four leading causes of poor sales for the independent business consultant.

Cause #1: Selling Is a Full-Time Job

Simply put, the mistake most consultants make is that they fail to recognize that they are *not* salespeople. Professional salespeople are just that—professionals, whose only role is to sell. Your role is to consult or coach, and sales becomes some sideline task you must do in order to fulfill your primary role. Look at any large and successful company and they know how important it is to have a dedicated sales force.

Salesmanship isn't just some collateral skill you pick up in order to become better at some other core job. It takes years of practice to become a very good salesperson. It takes a specific personality type as well. And it takes constant attention to keep that skill honed and sharp.

Treating sales as just another thing you need to accomplish in order to do your real job (i.e., consulting/coaching) will only result in mediocre results at best. Furthermore, thinking you can pick up sales in a few courses or as an ancillary skill simply won't work. Reading a few books on how to sell isn't going to get the job done either.

I know that everyone out there has probably told you that in order to grow your practice you need to sell, and I know this makes rational sense.

173

Unfortunately, until you realize that your core profession is being a consultant, not a salesperson, you will struggle.

Cause #2: Selling Isn't Right for What You Do

The key to understanding why you struggle with selling lies in understanding that you're borrowing best practices from the wrong role. You're using someone else's tools. It's like the carpenter borrowed your plumbing wrench to drive some nails. Just as assuming that the best sales techniques in retail will work for selling to the government is wrong, so too is it wrong to assume that the best sales practices of professional salespeople will work for you, the professional consultant.

Some consultants assume that they can just emulate other salespeople they've known. As executives in their former lives, they have had lots of exposure to salespeople trying to sell to them. Now that they themselves need to start selling, they try to copy what they saw other salespeople doing to them. It is like some perverse Golden Rule, "Do unto others as you have seen them do unto you." The only problem with this, though, is that in most cases the person you are trying to copy was a professional salesperson. You are not!

Even if you have been a professionally trained salesperson, the other reason you should stop playing "salesperson" is because you must be seen as the authority, the thought leader, or the expert. The moment you start selling, you undermine your prospect's belief in you *as the expert*. I know it isn't fair but the general perception of a salesperson is not that of a respectable authority or trusted advisor. I've been a very successful professional salesperson much of my life, so I know how false this stereotype is, but that doesn't change the fact that it still exists. The problem comes when you move from being a salesperson selling some other value proposition to being that value proposition yourself. In other words, when you become that which is being sold, the act of selling undermines your expertise.

What words come to mind if I ask you to describe a physician who called your house offering a free office visit? When I ask this in my classes the results are remarkable. With no more knowledge about the physician than this, the opinions range from, "not very good" and "bottom of his graduating class" to "hack" and even "he probably killed someone." Really? All this poor physician did was try to promote his business to you (by acting like the best salesperson he knew) and all of a sudden he is deemed incompetent, unethical, or worse.

Thought leaders and true experts are seen in a completely opposite light. Such figures enjoy the very opposite perception in the public eye. While neither perception may be justified, they exist nonetheless, and you must deal with this fact.

Cause #3: Selling Isn't Right for You

We've profiled over 600,000 people around the world and I can state with great confidence that there is definitely a set of natural talents or traits that lend themselves to success as either a sales professional or a consultant. The big problem is that the traits in each profession aren't the same. The traits that make a sales superstar are not the same traits that make a great consultant or coach.

So when I say that selling is "not right for who you are," I mean that your personality profile is probably much better aligned with being a consultant or coach than it is for being a salesperson. While there are always exceptions to any rule, the great majority of consultants I've certified have been much more ideally suited to do what they love to do (i.e., coach and consult) than filling the role of professional salesperson.

When you allow your success to become dependent on your non-talents (i.e., allowing your practice to depend on your sales talents), you have created a significant problem for your business. You've manufactured those weaknesses I discussed earlier, by allowing your practice's success to depend on your becoming the best salesperson—not the best consultant.

Cause #4: The "Die-chotomy" of Being an Independent Consultant

I realize I can't be an idealist. I appreciate that, as an independent, if you don't bring in new business you don't survive. I appreciate that you are the only one in the business and it falls on your shoulders to grow the practice. The real problem is, unlike any other sales role, *you are selling you.* The one doing the selling is you, but the thing being sold is also you. That's what I call the "die-chotomy" of being an independent consultant—having to be both the seller and that which is sold.

Now, if you are a follower of old-school sales training you may have heard that "you have to sell yourself" in sales. In reality, nothing could be further from the truth! In your world, trust is far more important than just being liked. It's not about being "liked," it's all about being "trusted." By taking any actions that position you as a salesperson in your prospect's mind, you erode their trust in you as the expert.

This is the very essence of the problem. The dichotomy of being both expert and salesperson will kill you in the end if you let it. Most consultants will die trying to be both, never realizing the opposing view that each role creates in the mind of their prospect. Bear in mind that they appreciate the salesperson's role to sell because he or she is the conduit to something the buyer wants. The key, however, is that the salesperson is not what the buyer wants, just the conduit to it. In your case, as the consultant, *you* are what they want to buy. When you take up the sales role you become both the product and the conduit to it, thus creating confusion and reducing the chances of the sale. The key to your success lies in your ability to pick just one of these two professions.

To overcome all of the problems above, you need to replace the sales techniques built for professional salespeople with a sales approach designed exclusively for professional consultants and coaches.

Most consultants follow the linear logic that says, "I need to sell more consulting, therefore I must sell; I must become a salesperson." The only flaw in this logic is that they fail to ever consider there could be another route to getting more business that doesn't require "selling" as it's classically defined.

In the next chapter I show you how to become comfortable being the consultant who gets more business instead of attempting to be the salesperson who tries to do the same.

8

He Who Identifies the Cause of the Problem Gets to Fix It

Becoming the Business Diagnostician

Business diagnostician is the term I use to remind me of my primary value in the sales process. It helps me remember that the most effective way to sell services to potential clients is to *not* try to sell to them at all. While every other consultant out there is trying to sell to that prospect, imagine how different and unique you will be when you seek first to help them identify the actual cause of their problem—and for free.

Many consultants create an artificial barrier to their success by placing the objective of selling in front of helping the client to improve their organization's overall condition. In reality, the primary objective with any prospect shouldn't be to "sell them"; rather, it should be to "solve them." Instead of focusing on selling solutions, seek first to identify the problem and its cause. When you do this, you will create an environment where that prospect sees you as the expert, has already received significant benefit from you, and you've avoided having to become a great salesperson; instead, you made your ability to acquire new business dependent on your expertise as a consultant, not a sales professional. Help the prospect understand the cause of their problem, and they will ask you for help.

At the very core of this chapter lies one of my most concrete personal mantras. I know of no other single statement that holds more potential to increase the profitability of your practice . . . period!

"He Who Identifies the Cause of the Problem Gets to Fix It"

Once you change your legacy thinking from "I need to sell" to one of "I need to diagnose," I guarantee you will be much more successful and much happier! It may seem like a subtle difference, but the impact of such a shift in thinking is immeasurable. The moment you learn to seek out helping prospects (yes, prospects, *not* paying clients) and identify the cause of their problems instead of going out and selling them services, you will witness significant growth in your practice. Making this your daily mantra will remind you of your true value proposition, keep you focused on the actions necessary to deliver that value, and steer you away from most distractions that will take you down the unsuccessful selling path.

It's vital that you understand that there is a cause and effect relationship between identifying the problem and being the one to fix it. In this relationship, the goal you are after is being paid to solve the problem. The cause of that effect, however, is that you identify what is actually creating that problem in the first place—before they become your client.

There are many reasons why a salesperson can hope they get the sale. Here are some of the most common reasons why consultants hope a prospect will hire them:

- Best price.
- Better marketing collateral.
- They related better with the prospect.
- Best credentials.
- Best references.
- They showed them the actual cause of their problem.

While all the causes above can be good, it is the last one that has the greatest effect on the prospect, and will deliver the most business. In addition, it is this last reason that is least likely to be replicated by your competition. There is no more powerful a reason to hire a consultant than for the simple fact that they have already identified what's causing the problem. Do that and they will ask you to help them fix it. Trust me!

I call this methodology the "diagnostic sales process." This process has been carefully learned and practiced by thousands of consultants over many years, and is the distillation of all the best practices I've seen those seven-figure consultants use to grow their businesses to such heights. It is so effective because it takes into consideration your role as the authority in the mind of your prospect.

It also takes into account the underlying psychology of the buyer, something most sales techniques do not do very well, if at all. Therefore, it's important that you understand a few basic truths about the underlying psychology of purchasing behavior that drives its effectiveness.

The Psychology of Sales

There are a lot of variables when it comes to selling. Hundreds of models exist, each with their own pros and cons, and there are a great many different kinds of sales as well.

The specific type of sale we're concerned with, however, is very well defined and deals specifically with selling consultative services. And when it comes to doing that, there are three basic truths about the psychology of sales that you must know.

Truth #1. The ABCs of Traditional Sales Must Be Rewritten

The old sales adage, "Always be closing" has existed for years, and if you are a professional salesperson, it's still a very good one because it keeps you centered on the core of your value proposition. This old-school approach only works, however, when what is expected of you in the eyes of your prospect is to sell. They know you are a salesperson so it's okay, and appropriate, to be seen this way. It's *not* okay to be seen in this way as a consultant since your primary value proposition better be to help them. They don't want you to sell to them; they want you to help fix them.

Instead of "closing," think "consulting" so that you will "Always be consulting" when you are in front of your prospect. Remember to also demonstrate your true value. Any time you interact with a prospect, remember not to sell them, just consult to them, because that's what they want from you and that's what they must experience.

> **Summary:** In the spirit of Truth #1, resist the urge to put on your sales cap and stick with wearing your consulting cap throughout any and all contacts with prospects.

Truth #2. The More You Connect, the More You Collect

While this is true in almost all types of sales, nowhere is it truer than in selling professional services like consulting or coaching. There is a direct positive correlation between how well you get to know your prospect and your ability to successfully offer them a solution they will accept. In short, the more you know about them, the more accurately you can identify the cause of their problem and therefore the more effectively you will turn them into clients.

Many consultants fail to really connect with the prospect. They get so focused on explaining their solutions, or selling their tools or services, that they fail to stop and question their way to the sale. Remember, an individual can only focus on one thing at a time and it's one of these four things:

1. You, the salesperson
2. Your product or service
3. Your organization
4. Themselves

Failing to keep the focus on #4 above (i.e., the prospect themselves) will lead you away from the sale, away from the core problem and away from success. There are times to focus on the other areas, but in selling consultative services, we've learned that the focus must stay on the prospect as much as possible.

Summary: Other sales processes take the focus off the prospect, whereas the diagnostic sales process keeps it squarely on the prospect at all times.

Truth #3. People Buy for Their Reasons, Not Yours

It's common sense that people are different. They each have their own buying motives, drivers, and interests. But, while it's not hard to remember this fact, it is really easy to forget it. Realizing that your prospect will only buy for their reasons, not your own, will drastically improve your results when it comes to converting prospects into paying clients.

To effectively garner trust and commitment from your prospects, you must replace what you think is important and how you like to communicate with what they think is important and how they prefer to communicate. A cornerstone of the diagnostic sales process involves a unique and foolproof way of securing this information about your prospect before you do anything else.

This model will give you a guaranteed way of knowing exactly what the prospect's strongest buying motives and communication style are so you aren't left assuming, guessing, or using your own as a basis.

Summary: Failing to accurately understand the drivers, motivations, and preferred communication style of the prospect is a sure-fire recipe for failure.

The Diagnostic Sales Process

Before we dive into the process I need to let you know up front that in order to use this process, just like any good physician, you will need to use some sort of diagnostic profile. There are a ton of them on the market. I will give you a list of the top seven I know and have used in Step #4 below. I don't know a single consultant who has developed a significantly profitable practice without using at least one form of measurement tool.

The Diagnostic Sales Process consists of five simple steps. They are:

Step #1—Induce your customers to come to you:
This is about replacing old-school push marketing with contemporary pull marketing techniques. Here, education-based marketing must replace sales-based marketing and you've already learned the 16 best vehicles to achieve this pull attraction.

Step #2—Establish a concrete power source:
The critical issue your prospect is struggling with drives everything. It is what keeps them up at night and what will become the source of power needed to fuel any call to action you will give them.

Step #3—Advance a hypothetical Cause:
These are the key variables that are actually causing the critical issue (i.e., power source). These variables must be measurable through some validated profile that measures personal competencies, natural talents, behavioral style, personality, and so on.

Step #4—Recommend diagnostic profiling:
This is where you actually apply that diagnostic tool, and schedule time to go over the findings.

Step #5—Negotiate the appropriate solution:
Based on the findings of your diagnostic profile work, you will make a recommendation to fix the cause of their problem. In other words, your proposal for consulting, training, coaching, and so on.

Each of these steps feeds directly into the next. By "walking this process" (i.e., taking your client through it step-by-step), you will hone in on the exact problem that will drive your successful sale. There is a natural progression to this model. It starts small and uses the client's own energy to drive to the next step. Word of caution: never skip a step. While you will be tempted, and the prospect will give you the signs (so you think) that they are ready to skip to the end and buy, for reasons you can't appreciate at this stage—*don't!*

The Physician Analogy

Before we walk through the steps of the diagnostic sales process, let me show you how it actually works in a way I know you've already experienced first hand. This approach isn't new to you; you've actually been on the receiving end of it before. To show you what I mean let's use the analogy of a trip to your physician's office.

Step #1. You have a pain in your knee so you schedule an appointment to see a physician. You don't respond to being pushed to a specific physician because she called your house. You were induced to reach out to this particular physician because of the education-based (pull) marketing that she has done in your local community. It may be through a referral from a trusted friend, or it may be because you've come to view this physician (or at least the medical group) as a respected authority in your area. Notice, however, how you would not be likely to choose the doctor you saw advertised on the back of the bus in front of you, or from the mailer flyer sent to your house. This is the equivalent of Step #1 (induce your customers to come to you) in the diagnostic sales process, and what you've already learned in those 16 marketing vehicles.

Step #2. You are sitting in the exam room and the physician walks in. Her first objective is to ascertain exactly what your pain is (e.g., where does it hurt, when does it hurt, how badly does it hurt, how long has it hurt, etc.). The key is that she will conduct a very thorough exam to make sure she has a complete understanding of the pain. What would you think of a doctor who walked into the room and started pitching you (e.g., "Hi, Mr. Smith, nice to meet you. I'd like to talk about our surgical solutions and how they could help you feel better.")? This is the equivalent of Step #2 (establish a concrete power source) in the diagnostic sales process.

Step #3. Your physician's next step is most likely to put forth some possible causes of your pain; the most common reasons why others have had similar pain (e.g., "Typically such pain is caused by a meniscal tear, Mr. Smith."). The importance of this step can't be overemphasized. Were she to jump straight from inquiring about your pain to recommending some surgery or treatment, you would feel she is taking action without knowing the full story. Putting forth a hypothetical cause is vital, in order to establish herself as an authority in your eyes. Psychologically, this reinforces her expertise.

Now, the key is what she does next. Any good physician would never act on a "possible cause" without first verifying or proving that such a cause really is to blame. And, like 99 percent of all patients, you would gladly comply with her recommendations to do further testing, because you want to stop the pain. This is the equivalent of Step #3 (advise them of possible causative metrics) in the diagnostic sales process.

Step #4. So, you get your MRI and find yourself back in the physician's office anxiously waiting for her to go over the findings. Your doctor brings with her the actual results from the MRI and displays them for you to see with your own eyes. While you don't really have any idea what the images mean, your physician does and that's all that matters. As she interprets the results of your diagnostic tests she tells you (and more importantly shows you) what is and isn't correct. The key here is that even though you (the prospect) don't understand the results, you believe your physician much more because she showed you something tangible. This is the equivalent of Step #4 (recommend diagnostic profiling) in the diagnostic sales process.

Step #5. Finally, having come to believe in your physician as the knowledgeable expert she is, you come to the point where you look at her and ask, "So, how do we fix it, Doc"? With absolute conviction you trust her advice and actively (desperately perhaps) seek it out. She doesn't have to sell you on anything. Quite the opposite, you find yourself *asking* for her help and recommendation.

This is the equivalent to Step #5 (negotiate the appropriate solution) in the diagnostic sales process.

Unbeknownst to you, you just witnessed the diagnostic sales process in action. Every step, every cause, every effect, and every nuance perfectly fits the exact process, as you're about to learn it.

The real key to the diagnostic sales process is this: Whereas old sales techniques seek to get the prospect to take something from you, this technique gets them to ask you to give them something.

Don't be deceived by the similarity in these statements. The former is push marketing and sales and doesn't work very well. The latter is perfect pull marketing and consulting. When you turn the process around and create a situation where your prospect asks for your advice or recommendation, the odds of them accepting it skyrocket! Go back to your visit to the doctor and view it in a sales perspective. You weren't being sold a solution, you were *asking* for one.

Now that you have a better appreciation for the psychological underpinnings that make this process work, let's dive in.

Induce the Customer to Come to You

As we've discussed, traditional sales-based marketing just doesn't work well anymore. It is especially poor in your profession as a consultant. It alienates the prospect, positions you as a salesperson, attempts to push on the rope and, in the end, takes you farther away from where you want to be, not closer.

However, everything you've learned prior to this point about how to market using education-based principles in all 16 marketing vehicles is designed to induce prospects to come to you. As long as you practice everything I've already taught you about your marketing, you will successfully achieve Step #1 in this process and prospects will come to you. Everything from here on out is what you need to do once they arrive.

Establish a Concrete Power Source

The power source is the critical issue in the mind of your prospect that drives everything. It is what keeps them up at night and it will be the source of power needed to fuel any call to action you decide to give them.

The reason I call this the power source, by the way, is two-fold. First, it's easy to get off track and start focusing on the solution too early. Delivering training, consulting, or coaching is only a means to an end. It is the power source (or correcting it) that should always be the end objective. Actions mean nothing—only results matter—so don't start focusing on the actions you hope to sell too early. Using this term helps you to remember to always remain focused on solving the core problem first.

Second, I use the term *Power Source* because eventually you will be giving them a call to action, and action requires energy. The thing that will drive their actions is their pain or desire, so by remembering that their pain is the power source, you will always remember to connect any call to action you give them with the source that will power it.

All power sources should have two key things well fleshed out—a quantity and a quality:

- **A financial impact (the quantity)**—It's vital that you establish an actual monetary impact of the core problem. Doing so helps you better understand the scope of the issue and it will be instrumental when you move to your proposal phase. Also, there is one pretty cool little side effect of getting this information. It actually helps to further position you as the expert. If the prospect has a concrete answer for this question, great. However, believe it or not, more often than not my prospects don't have a solid answer when it comes to the question of exactly what this issue is literally costing them. While I seek to establish this for my own benefit as much as theirs, I've found that by helping them answer this question before we go any further, I've shown them something that they didn't really know and the impression on the prospect is, "Hmm, if he is already helping us understand the problem much better here and now, how much more value can he provide once we start to actually pay him?"
- **An emotional impact (the quality)**—It is equally as important to make sure you get some emotional costs qualified as well. Many times it's not the financial ramifications that will drive the sale, it's the emotional toll. For example, in addition to the big money being lost on this one salesperson, the business owner you are talking with is equally as concerned for the security of his business, paying for his kid's college, or what happens to his family if revenue doesn't increase. It is these emotions that will drive more action than anything else.

Once you establish this power source you have something to plug into when you request action in your proposal stage later on. It's incumbent on you to know where that power will come from, not the prospect. Also, make sure you have their biggest issue. The bigger the power source, the bigger the call to action can be (i.e., the larger the proposal they will act on).

Once you feel you have a thorough enough understanding of exactly what the biggest problem is, and its financial and emotional ramifications, you're ready to move to the next step in the process.

Advance a Hypothetical Cause

This is the number one most neglected step by most consultants, and the number one reason a sale never materializes.

A hypothetical cause is your statement about what you feel the typical variables are that could be causing the prospect's problem. The key is that any cause you put forth needs to be—must be—measurable. You can't diagnose a cause with speculation, guesswork, or subjective opinion. That's the problem with too many consultants. They fail to get the buy-in that their solution will work because they haven't actually shown the prospect that they *know* what's causing the problem, and can *show* that cause tangibly. Go back to your visit to your physician. How much more likely are you to take her advice and schedule major surgery if she either never tested anything, or did but didn't bother to show you any results? I'm not talking about minor medication treatments like prescribing some antibiotic, nor am I talking about some minor consultative solution either. If you want to get big engagements, you need big action, which requires a big buy-in centered around solving a big power source. It's all about turning something intangible into something tangible and real for the prospect. Do this and they will believe in you and your recommendation.

Let's take a look at some examples of this step in action:

- **Example #1:** Power source = poor sales. I advise the prospect that one of the most common causes for poor sales performance is a salesperson who doesn't possess the natural talents proven to exist in the very best salespeople. Specifically, they may not have natural talents for: self-starting ability, competitiveness, personal work ethic, decisiveness, and emotional intelligence. Now, while I do know that these are some of the hallmark traits of the very best salespeople, I do not in fact know whether or not these traits are absent in the underperforming salespeople. Being the "why guess when we can know" guy that I am, I recommend the prospect let me give a free sales profile to one of their worst salespeople and let's just see.

- **Example #2:** Power source = poor leadership. I advise the prospect that one of the most common causes of poor leaders is a lack of key leadership traits like emotional intelligence, strategic thinking, problem solving, sense of authority, and humility. As in the last example, I let the prospect know that I'm confident that these traits drive superior leaders, but I do not know if their absence is what's causing her leaders to be so poor. I go back to the "why guess when we can know," offer a free online leadership skills assessment, and we're off to the races.

It builds confidence in your prospect's mind when you are able to offer up likely causes of their pain. Better yet, your first recommendation isn't some expensive solution. You move the relationship deeper and further slowly, by asking for small steps. In this case, small free steps. I don't remember the last time a prospect turned down the opportunity to answer the burning question I just created in their head of, "I wonder if *that's* the cause of my pain"? For ten minutes to complete a free diagnostic profile that would give me an answer to that question, why wouldn't I do it?

Final thought on this step: Be sure to always ask the prospect what they think the cause is before you advance your own. I do this mostly because it's polite and good business etiquette, but sometimes they actually have some good ideas. In all but the rarest of cases the difficulty doesn't lie in accurately knowing the cause and not knowing how to fix it, but rather the problem normally lies in not understanding the true cause in the first place.

Here's a more complete example of what a conversation might look like at this stage in the process.

Well, Mr. Smith, do you have any ideas as to what's causing this problem. Hmm, that's definitely a possibility. I've coached hundreds of sales professionals and in my experience, in addition to what you just said, some of the even more common causes of poor sales are: call reluctance, lack of emotional intelligence, or a lack of aggressive closing. Of course, I couldn't be sure any of these were the real cause behind John's poor sales performance until I actually measure them. While I've got some strong suspicions that a couple of these are behind the problem, given what you've said about John, I'd like to give John a diagnostic profile that is specifically designed to measure these kinds of sales traits and then we'll know for sure. As I always say, "why guess when you can know." I don't charge for these tests, by the way, because until I know what the cause of the problem is, I don't know if I have any solutions to offer, so it's just as much of a benefit for me to know as it is for you. It's a simple online profile that takes 10 to 15 minutes to complete and I'm the only one who would see the results (which I would share with you, of course). Being able to identify traits will allow me to help explain the real reason behind why sales are down $450,000.

Let's stop here and break this statement down, because there are some absolutely vital pieces to it that, were you to leave them out, would reduce your success rate drastically.

1st Segment: *"Well, Mr. Smith, do you have any ideas as to what's causing this problem (listen, listen, listen). Hmm, that's definitely a possibility. I've coached hundreds of sales professionals and in my experience, in addition to what you said, some of the even more common causes of poor sales are: call reluctance, lack of emotional intelligence, an inability to adequately connect with the customer, or possibly a lack of aggressive closing."*

First ask them what they think the cause is to be polite and professional. Acknowledge their thoughts, but then introduce your own hypothetical cause. The key objective here is to create that psychological belief that you will identify the cause of the problem at hand. Notice how I establish credibility by letting the prospect know I've coached hundreds of people in this situation. This is where you state three or four likely traits that might be missing and causing the problem. Don't worry at this point because in the coming section I will teach you where to go to learn all of the traits that profiles actually measure.

2nd Segment: *"Of course, I couldn't be sure any of these were the real cause behind John's poor sales performance until I actually measure them. While I've got some strong suspicions that a couple of these are behind the problem, given what you've said about John, I'd like to give John a diagnostic profile that is specifically designed to measure these kinds of sales traits—then we'll know for sure. As I always say, why guess when you can know."*

The key objective here is to demonstrate your professionalism and ethics by not jumping at the sale. You're the expert and you won't make irrational judgments to recommend solutions until you know what needs to be fixed first. I can't tell you how many times your competition will not follow this step and jump at the chance to recommend a solution or switch into sales mode. One of our most successful consultant teams, Bryan Arzani and Jennifer Erickson, serves as a great example of this. They were up against several other consulting firms for a really big contract. While the competition jumped at recommendations for this or that, Bryan and Jennifer stopped to say that they should identify the actual cause first, before suggesting anything to the bidding company. When they won the business the client told them, "We decided on you because you were the only one who didn't jump at selling a solution, but rationally stopped to partner with us in making sure we did it right."

3rd Segment: *"I don't charge for these tests, by the way, because until I know what the cause of the problem is, I don't know if I have any solutions to offer, so it's just as much of a benefit for me to know as it is for you. It's a simple online profile that takes 10 to 15 minutes to complete and I'm the only one who would see the results (which I would share with you, of course)."*

The key objective here is to remove any obstacles or barriers that automatically pop up in the prospect's mind relating to costs. Why let some $150 profile block the path for your $20,000 consulting gig? Also, and more importantly, it prevents them from seeing you as a salesperson whose ulterior motive is really just to sell them a profile.

4th Segment: *"Being able to identify traits will allow me to help explain the real reason behind why sales are down $450,000."*

The key here is to connect back to the power source. You're not asking them to take action for action's sake. Remember that the power source is what drives (powers) action. You worked to define it, now put it to use. Plug into that power source directly by making sure they keep focused on the fact that anything you're asking them to do is to solve their big problem. I do that by *always* ending any sentence where I ask for action with a restatement of the main problem or power source and specifically the financial pain if possible. If you don't "plug the call to action in," you may not find any action.

Now that you've adequately explored the problem and sufficiently understand what it is, you're ready to move to Step Four and actually conduct some diagnostic testing.

Recommend Diagnostic Profiling

This step involves selecting and recommending the specific diagnostic profile that you will use to actually quantify the variables and help you diagnose the cause of the critical issue.

This may come as a bit of a surprise to you, but in reality you are in the human element business. I say this because an organization is literally defined as "a group of *people* organized around a common objective." While there are processes and equipment, everything in any organization revolves around the humans who set and follow those processes, and who design, buy, manufacture, or use that equipment. As such, understanding the human element is one of the most important things any consultant can do.

I have a personal belief that states: "All organizational performance is generated between the ears."

This means that any objective in the organization eventually comes back to one or more people and what is happening in their heads. This is why understanding the human element is so vital to improving any business result.

I've seen a great many consultants struggle to be successful because they chose to focus on the things those humans work with, or how they work with them (i.e., things or processes), yet failed to fully consider the human element that actually drives them. I'm not talking about Human

Resource work mind you. Not at all! Not that I have anything against HR departments, per se, but all of my work is with top executives, whose primary concerns are for efficiency, revenue, performance, and profits. Understanding the people responsible for delivering such things is a means to an end. Knowing this, let's look at what options you have for understanding that human element better by using diagnostic tools. I recommend you consider using these broad categories of such tools:

- **Behavioral profiles:** Tools that measure a person's natural behavioral style, which controls strengths and weaknesses for a wide array of tasks, duties, abilities, and preferences. Identifying that an individual doesn't have the ability or aptitude for lots of detailed work, empathy, being assertive or a self-starter, for example, can be vital in understanding why they aren't performing. Such profiles literally measure a person's ability to do the actual job.
- **Motivational profiles:** Tools that measure a person's core motivations, their passions, and what will get them ultimately engaged in their work. Having key drivers that are not being satisfied is a common cause of lack of engagement, dissatisfaction at work, poor work ethic, and voluntary turnover issues. Such profiles actually measure how much someone likes or loves to do the work.
- **Organizational profiles:** Tools that, instead of measuring individual traits, measure the actual organization's performance in a number of broad categories like sales and marketing, customer service, management, teams, and so on. For those of you not consulting on human issues, this category of diagnostic tool allows you to create your own criteria to be assessed, thus allowing you to still diagnose the health of your prospect's organization and effectively use this methodology.

All of these tools are very accurate nowadays. This wasn't as true only 10 or more years ago perhaps, but modern science and technology have improved their validity and reliability to degrees approaching 95 percent. They are all available online and are very easy to learn and use effectively. In this book I'm going to educate you on the profiles my own company has created because we've designed them specifically to fit this model, but so as not to be biased, here's a list of other publishers you can check out and consider using as well. Each of them provides highly accurate, very well proven, and user-friendly profiles, along with simple means of learning how to apply them:

- Innermetrix Incorporated (www.innermetrix.com)—my own company
- The Platinum Rule (www.platinumrule.com)
- People Keys (www.peoplekeys.com)
- Maximum Potential (www.maximumpotential.com)
- Profiles International (www.profilesinternational.com)
- Inscape Publishing (www.inscapepublishing.com)
- Extended Disc (www.extendeddisc.com)

Whichever provider you choose, make sure you can get access to an *unlimited* license rather than paying per report. If you have to pay $25 to $30 per report (which is typical), you are restricted in using them effectively in both your marketing vehicles and in the diagnostic sales process. Even if you could get away with charging a nominal fee to cover expenses in the sales process, there is no way to do so in the marketing programs.

I learned this the hard way in my own company because we used to charge a per-report price. We switched to an unlimited, per-month flat rate, specifically because those consultants told us it was too cost prohibitive. Your ability and willingness to prolifically use them as I described in the marketing vehicles relies on you not having to worry about paying anything extra if 1,000 potential clients read your article and show up at your webinar.

Behavioral Profiles

When it comes to behavioral profiles I choose to follow the work of famed Harvard psychologist William Marston. His DISC theory of behavioral style is the most widely accepted and used theory in business today. Our version of the DISC behavioral profile is called the DISC Index. By using the DISC Index, you can measure the following 48 behavioral traits:

Ability to relate to others	Forcefulness
Ability to support others	Generosity
Acceptance to change	Impulsiveness
Accuracy	Independence
Adventure	Inquisitiveness
Aggressiveness	Introversion
Assertiveness	Modesty
Attention to detail	Organization
Carefulness	Passivity
Cautiousness	Patience
Charm	Perfectionism
Competitiveness	Persuasiveness
Conscientiousness	Poise
Consistency	Practicality
Cooperativeness	Precision
Decisiveness	Rebelliousness
Defiance	Reliability
Degree of optimism	Restlessness
Degree of pessimism	Results orientation
Dependability	Risk aversion
Determination	Spontaneity
Enthusiasm	Stability
Extroversion	Stubbornness
Flexibility	Teamwork orientation

Figure 8.1 demonstrates the way the DISC Index visually displays these traits.

It's the ability to quantify these kinds of intangibles for your prospects that helps explain why any one individual is struggling with performance. Just read back through this list with the question, "How would this affect performance if it was not present, or in some

Decisive	Interactive	Stabilizing	Cautious
Problems:	People:	Pace:	Procedures:
How you tend to approach problems and make decisions	How you tend to interact with others and share opinions	How you prefer to pace things in your environment	Your preference for established protocol/standards
High D	High I	High S	High C
Demanding	Gregarious	Patient	Cautious
Driving	Persuasive	Predictable	Perfectionist
Forceful	Inspiring	Passive	Systemic
Daring	Enthusiastic	Complacent	Careful
Determined	Sociable	Stable	Analytical
Competitive	Poised	Consistent	Orderly
Responsible	Charming	Steady	Neat
Inquisitive	Convincing	Outgoing	Balanced
Conservative	Reflective	Restless	Independent
Mild	Matter-of-fact	Active	Rebellious
Agreeable	Withdrawn	Spontaneous	Careless
Unobtrusive	Aloof	Impetuous	Defiant
Low D	Low I	Low S	Low C

Figure 8.1   The DISC Index Traits

cases was?" Imagine the sales person who lacks assertiveness, or another one who has too much forcefulness. How effective would an administrative assistant be without great attention to detail? Would a risk-averse employee deal with upheaval and change very well?

Motivational Profiles

To measure an individual's motivational preferences, their passions, and key drivers of engagement, we've built the Values Index around the research of Dr. Eduard Spranger, whose theories on motivation and engagement are among the most applied in the world. Using the Values Index you can measure for the following 38 motivators:

Acquisition of knowledge	Independence
Aesthetics	Influence
An improved society	Leadership
Artistic expression	Learning opportunities
Authority	Logic
Autonomy	Maximizing gains
Balance and harmony	Monetary gains
Benefit to others	Mutual respect
Best value for money	Power/Control
Caring	Practical returns
Compassion	Regulation/Processes
Competitive edge	Rules/Order over chaos
Creativity	Self-fulfillment
Discovering the truth	Selflessness
Efficiency	Status and esteem
Ethics/Principles	Systems/Structure
Form over function	Traditional ways
Generating value/revenue	Uniqueness
Generosity	Utility/Functionality

Figure 8.2 is a sample of the seven motivational categories measured in the Values Index.

Being able to accurately understand what motivates a person at this level of granularity helps determine if someone will be well satisfied in any given culture or role. Motivations and passions drive engagement, which is a significant driver of performance. Imagine someone motivated by an independent working structure reporting to a micromanaging supervisor. Conversely, what might be the odds of someone motivated by systems and structure being demotivated in a role where they've been given extreme freedom? And, how successful will an organization be when they decide to completely revamp their entire process to modernize for environmental reasons, yet 75 percent of the staff are motivated by tradition and stability? While for all the right reasons, the company unfortunately just alienated the majority of their workforce.

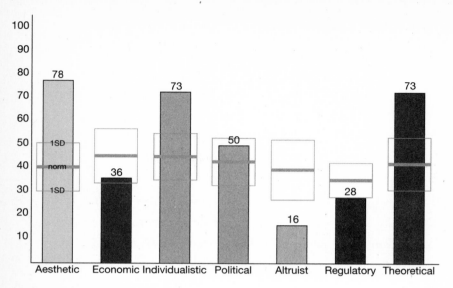

Figure 8.2   The Values Index

Organizational Profiles

While I still believe that all performance is generated between the ears, many times you need to view the aggregate of that human performance on an organizational level. The Organizational Health Checkup (OHC) allows leaders in the organization to evaluate the company's performance in these core areas:

- Personal—How do the individuals in your organization feel in general?
- Employee Alignment—Is everyone driving for results and profits?
- Personnel—How effectively do you lead people?
- Team Effectiveness—How strong are your teams?
- Leadership—How trusted and inspiring is your leadership?
- Strategy and Planning—How comprehensive and secure is your strategy?
- Customer Service—How loyal are your customers?
- Sales and Marketing—Does your pitch resonate and do your people sell?
- Operations—Do you run efficient and quality operations?

- Cultural—How cohesive and beneficial is your culture?
- Management—How effectively do you manage things?

Figure 8.3 shows how these 11 dimensions are displayed in the OHC. Higher scores represent better performance.

The OHC is very good at doing two things as far as the consultant is concerned. First, it expands my reach, meaning I may meet one executive, but since this is a tool designed to gauge performance as viewed by multiple executive viewpoints, it's a perfect reason to get involved with other leaders. Second, it engineers epiphanies. As surprising as it might seem to some, anyone with senior management or consulting experience will not be surprised to find that many leaders don't all share the same opinion concerning performance in key indicators like these. Aggregating a group of management's opinions and combining them like this often results in an "aha moment" when the leadership team realizes they have a problem. Of course it doesn't

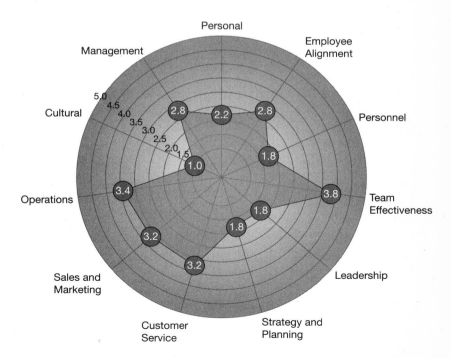

Figure 8.3 The Eleven Dimensions of the Organizational Health Checkup

hurt to be the only outside consultant in the room when they have this epiphany.

To help any class of business consultant utilize this diagnostic sales process I've also created a customizable organizational profile. It is based on the OHC but instead of measuring the predetermined eleven categories I focus on, you can customize your own set of categories and diagnostic questions. Let's say you have a program in your consulting business that examines the "5 dimensions of financial health." This tool allows you to customize the OHC profile to your specific categories (i.e., your 5 dimensions), title them what you want, and create a set of diagnostic questions for each category (e.g., "Every employee is familiar with all Federal regulations regarding fiscal reporting," or "We consistently strive to reduce risk and secure our client's confidential information"). I've done this so even if it doesn't make sense in your consulting practice to diagnose human problems, or use behavioral or motivational diagnostic profiles, you can still benefit from this sales model simply by creating your own set of items to diagnose with your unique prospects. To check it out simply visit www.inner metrix.com and find the "Customizable OHC" under the resources tab.

The key thing to remember is that everything I just said about all three classes of profiles revolves around sales and marketing, not working with actual clients. Diagnostic metrics like these are incredibly powerful tools in helping you secure the actual business.

To learn more about any of these specific profiles visit www.innermetrix.com, and check out the "resources" tab.

Negotiate the Appropriate Solution

Here, in this final step, you will be debriefing the actual report you chose and making your recommendation for action, all in the same step. In other words, showing them the cause of the problem and proposing the appropriate solution (e.g., consulting, training, coaching).

The reason I put the actual debriefing of the profile in this step, and not in the previous step, is because you want to tie the debrief together with the recommendation, back to back. This is because the prospect's most powerful buying emotions will exist immediately after discovering the cause of the problem. The prospect is the most excited at this point. The buy-in they have for your expertise is the greatest at this point because you just showed them the cause of their problem; something that has plagued them for perhaps a very long time and something no one else has been able to do.

From a functional standpoint, it's also very timely due to the simple fact that it is at this point (i.e., during the debrief of the profile results) that most people give you their big buying signs. That buying signal usually comes in the form of a question (e.g., "So how do we fix that?" or "What can be done to solve that?"). Any question about how to resolve the cause of the problem is, in effect, a buying sign. So, putting the debrief and recommendation together makes the most sense because instead of having to switch into sales mode your recommendation is simply in response to their request for assistance.

In all the work I've done with consultants I've certified, literally 90 percent of the time when they debrief a report with a prospect in this process, that person ends up asking a "buy-sign" question. This is what I was talking about in the beginning of this chapter when I said the key to the success of this model is moving away from the old-school sales mentality of asking a prospect to take something from you, and turning it around where they ask you to give them something instead.

Let's discuss the debrief portion of this step first. When I am debriefing a profile to a prospect I give a very different debrief than I would if I were going over the profile with a coaching client. Where I could easily spend up to an hour or more debriefing a profile for an existing client, with a prospect I might only spend 10 to 20 minutes maximum. The reason for this is that when dealing with a prospect, I'm not going to do all the education I would with an actual client.

The reason behind why I'm going over the profile is vastly different between a prospect and an actual client. In the case of an actual client, I'm using the profile information as part of the coaching or developmental work I've already been hired to provide. It's a much more involved relationship and they've already paid me to provide it. With a prospect, however, I'm using the profile for one simple reason—to identify the cause of their problem, and elicit one of those "buy-sign" questions.

Because of this, I simply give them a very high-level overview of what the profile looks at and isolate just those variables that point to a cause. It's actually a good thing if they say they want more under-standing of the results, because my response at that point is, "That's understandable, Mr. Smith, and while my main objective here was to show you that I've identified these traits as a cause of the problem, once we get into the program I recommend we will definitely go deeper into the profile's results." Psychologically, this starts to create the assumption and perspective that working together is a bit of a foregone conclusion, and starts them thinking "when" not "if."

Here's an example of a debrief introduction with a prospect:

Hi, Mr. Smith, and thanks for having John complete the profile. While this profile could be the center of many weeks' worth of coaching, for our purposes here let's just look at what I see with regard to John's poor sales performance. This graph shows us that he has a very low level of what we call decisiveness, which means that he may not be comfortable thinking on his feet or acting decisively out in the field when handed a curve ball. Also, this graph (very high C in the DISC profile) tells me that John is likely to be a perfectionist and overly detailed. Another thing I noticed is that John has a very low drive for financial compensation (economics on the Values Index is in last place). In my experience, this can cause a lot of problems for salespeople because their passion has less to do with making commissions and more to do with, in John's case, helping others (he had a high Altruistic drive). By simply meeting with the prospect and supporting their needs, he may not need to move all the way to the actual sale to satisfy his greatest motivation, or driver. So, in summary, I think we see in John someone whose natural talents and motivations are not supporting his success in sales right now. I can clearly see why he is struggling!

Stop here for a minute. If you were on the receiving end of the statements above, what odds would you place on the very next question you would want to ask being something along the lines of, "Okay, so how do we fix this?" or "So how do we develop these traits in John, and what would motivate him more completely?" My guess is that this is exactly the kind of question you already found yourself asking, and now you can see how even in a written example like this I was able to move from asking you to take something from me, to getting you to want to ask me to give you something (e.g., a recommendation for how to fix John in this case).

Once I get to the point where you have that burning question in your mind, as the prospect, I've achieved my goals. Now I simply answer your question. That answer will be whatever service or program I sell that will best address your question (e.g., sales training, leadership development, coaching, etc.).

Connecting the Dots

Regardless of the length of your debrief, there is one thing you must always make sure to do. You have to connect the dots between what you see in the report and what the prospect sees in reality. Better put, you have to let the prospect connect the dots for you. Each trait or item that I point to in the profile needs to be clearly connected to the problem in your prospect's mind. For example:

- **An unconnected example:** "Johnny has a low score in emotional intelligence, which means he isn't good with understanding others."
- **A connected example:** "Johnny has a low score in emotional intelligence, which means he probably struggles to truly understand his prospect's emotional state, or know when to go for the close or not, which would likely hurt his ability to sell."
- **An unconnected example:** "Jenny isn't great at strategic planning, so she probably struggles with conceptual thinking."
- **A connected example:** "Jenny isn't great at strategic planning, which would get in her way when it comes to leading and effectively planning and organizing her department's objectives."

The difference in a connected statement is I always tie the profile results directly to the power source for the prospect, not leave it up to them to do by themselves. And I don't want to leave the prospect in charge of the sale, ever. I want to make sure they see the connection between cause and effect.

If you're not sure how the results in the profile connect to the problem at hand, partner with the prospect right then and there to find out. You describe what the low score means in general, and ask them to help you understand how important that is for the role. Here are some examples of how that would work:

"Johnny has a low score in emotional intelligence, which means he isn't great at understanding others. How important is this kind of talent in the sales role he fills, Mr. Smith?"

"Jenny isn't great at strategic planning, so help me understand, Ms. Smith, how important strategic planning and complex problem solving are in Jenny's leadership role."

When used this way all you have to do is learn what the profile measures, which is very straightforward, and the profile will actually tell you what their score means. Then play the role of facilitator and ask the prospect to help connect that ability (or lack thereof) to the role for you. The end effect is every bit the same as if you knew the role very well yourself. We see 90 percent buy-sign questions either way.

And when those buy signs come, the only thing left to do is make your recommendation and ask for the close.

Don't Forget to Close

Having thoroughly given the act of selling the boot, there is actually one aspect of selling that you just can't get rid of—the actual close. Not that I'm advocating the use of some canned closing technique, but, if you never ask for the business, it won't come.

Even if you elicit the buy-sign questions 90 percent of the time, and make your recommendation for training or coaching, if all you do is say "I recommend sales training for Johnny," then thank the prospect for their time, hand them your card, and tell them to give you a call if they ever need sales training, you've wasted both their time and yours.

The key, however, is that you make a literal call to action with your recommendation, not just some ethereal suggestion. Sounds silly? You'd be surprised how many times a month I hear someone tell me, "I don't understand, Jay. I debriefed the report. I gave them everything and at the end there was this sort of 'what now' moment and they said they would get back to me and they never did." When I asked these consultants what recommendation they made, they said "none." And the prospect didn't call you back? Shocker! I bet that when you go fishing the fish don't jump into your boat for you either.

In effect, the prospect did exactly what these consultants asked for—nothing! They recommended nothing; the prospect did nothing.

Look, at this point in the game you've developed something of a super power. You may not be aware of it, but if you've executed these steps correctly you have the newfound ability to influence their decision-making with no less scary an influence than a Jedi knight (think "these aren't the droids you are looking for"). Whatever suggestion you make, they are more than likely to comply. I know this sounds crazy and you're probably thinking of examples in your life where you made a suggestion to a prospect and they completely didn't do it. My guess, though, is that you are thinking of an example where you were selling, weren't you? Selling is like kryptonite to your super powers. If you have stayed true to the lessons of this process, however, they will listen.

Here's a great rule of thumb to help you close the business without closing the door altogether. I like to think of it as the "You Asked Close." Whatever you say, whatever your call to action is, simply make the statement as if the prospect was already a paying client.

Basically, the "You Asked Close" is simply you making a recommendation, but with a real call to action, not just theory. Don't forget, everything you've done so far in this process has been carefully crafted to get you to the point where they ask you for the business. So give it to them!

Here are some great examples of "You Asked" closes. It is the last sentence that is the true "close" or call to action:

"Well, Mr. Smith, since you asked, I think the best way to get Johnny selling again would be to put him through a sales training program that helps develop his skills in these low areas. If you'd like I could talk about exactly how to do that with you, so his sales can start improving quickly."

"Sure thing, Ms. Johnson, you're correct. If you want Jenny to become a much stronger leader, she's going to have to learn what her strengths and weaknesses are and improve not only her abilities here, but how to pay extra attention to those weaknesses so she doesn't let them get in her way. I'd like to recommend you let me coach her through my leadership development program so we can stem the turnover below her and improve results in her department."

Please take note of how I connect the recommendation to the power source again. You must *always* connect any request for action to the power source!

It's in this recommendation that the work you did in Step #1 comes back to support you greatly. By making sure you did a great job of quantifying and qualifying the power source, you have a gauge as to what price to charge for this recommendation. Whatever solution you recommend, there will be a price tag on it. The funny thing about buying psychology, however, is that our simple reptilian brains are very much driven by our emotions. In fact, according to Professor Zaltman's research at Harvard University, as much as 90 percent of our purchasing decisions are controlled exclusively by our emotions, not by rational decision-making.

So, if your proposal has a tangible price and their problem doesn't— you're in trouble. If you compare the tangible price of your proposal to the tangible price of their problem, however, you should always be able to make a compelling emotional argument.

For example, your coaching program will cost the client $5,000 a month. If you imagine an old-fashioned scale and all you do is load your $5,000 price on one side, and all that exists on the opposite side is some ethereal, nondescript, intangible problem (e.g., "poor leadership"), then you have a problem. If you imagine that money has a weight to it, and the problem side of the scale is undefined and has not been qualified to a specific monetary value, your side of the scale will always weigh more (which is a bad thing). That would look something like Figure 8.4.

To make it easier for the prospect to agree to your recommendation, you would want your side of the scale to weigh nothing compared to the problem side. You want your side to have $5,000 on the one side and their $100,000 in lost sales on the other side. If you expand this to include all variables (emotions, at risk, etc.) you would have something more like Figure 8.5.

You need to have something tangible on both sides of the equation, and then make sure that your side weighs a hell of a lot less. This is just another version of the old saying, "It will cost a lot more not to fix it."

In general, the mistake most salespeople, let alone consultants, make is to assume the prospect will fill in their side of the scale themselves. Again, letting the prospect control the sale is never a

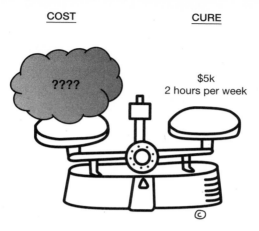

Figure 8.4 The Cost/Cure Scale

good idea. If you haven't defined the problem specifically enough to arrive at a real dollar and emotional amount, the prospect isn't likely to either. In the end, all their emotional mind sees is "some undefined value" on the one side of the scale, and "*five thousand dollars*" on the other. And that's just a small proposal. Imagine how much more important this balancing act is when you deliver a $50,000 to $100,000 proposal.

"In the absence of any recommendation, one finds the absence of any action."

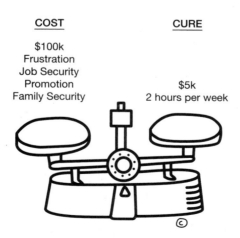

Figure 8.5 The Completed Cost/Cure Scale

Just don't forget. You can't push clients into the sale; you have to earn it. You must earn their respect as a trusted advisor. You have to earn their belief in your expertise. When done correctly I like to say, "I *EARNed* their business," as opposed to "I sold them an engagement."

How I *EARNed* the business:

- Induce the customer to come to you.
- Establish a concrete power source.
- Advance a hypothetical cause.
- Recommend diagnostic profiling.
- Negotiate the appropriate solution.

This is the diagnostic sales process. Once you learn it I think you'll be surprised how naturally it comes to you. The trick is forgetting all the bad sales techniques you've learned over the years and just focus on being the consultant. When you do this, sales will follow naturally. Figure out the cause of their problem and I guarantee they will ask you how to fix it!

The only thing you need to get started on using this process is to go get yourself some form of diagnostic profile. Check out the resources I gave you in section four of this chapter. It's absolutely critical that you have something here, so go figure that out now.

To help you put all of this together I've included a complete dialogue in the appendix that represents a sample conversation with a prospect, from beginning to end.

9

The Golden Rule Is Just Plain Wrong

Effective Communication = Effective Persuasion

If, when having any discussion with any prospect or client, you fail to actually communicate effectively (i.e., the words coming out of your mouth conflict with their preferred means of communicating), those words may fall on deaf ears. In fact, it's possible that your way of communicating may actually repel your prospect.

In communicating with another person, the Golden Rule (i.e., "Do unto others as you would have them do unto you") is completely wrong. As Dr. Tony Allessandra points out, "You can't always communicate with others in the way you like to be communicated with." What you need to do is to communicate with others the way they would like to be communicated to.

Here's a basic fact. Everyone has his or her own unique communication style. Based on their natural behavioral style they prefer to receive information in a fairly specific way. Failing to understand what that style is and how you need to factor it into your communications will make a huge difference in how effectively you sell to, and even work with, your clients.

In addition to a unique communication style, everyone also has his or her own unique buying motivation. Trying to compel a prospect to buy for your reasons just doesn't work.

Both of these factors, buying style and buying motive, are at play in every single person you meet and will try to sell to. This is one of the main reasons I champion using the DISC Index and Values Index as your diagnostic profiles. The DISC Index measures behavioral style, which equates to preferred communication style or "buying style." The Value Index measures motivations and passions, or "buying motive."

The great news is that by using these profiles up front with a prospect, for a totally different reason (i.e., identifying the *cause* of their pain), you get to enjoy the significant side effect of learning their buying motives and communication preferences. By knowing these things, and incorporating them into your approach, you will drastically increase your ability to EARN. more business.

The Seven Buying Motives (Why People Buy)

Dr. Eduard Spranger conducted years of research into what drives a person, and motivates them. He determined that regardless of how people described their motivations, there were seven core dimensions into which all of these descriptions fell. By understanding what motivates the prospect, you can understand what value to highlight in your solution.

For example, imagine you are selling leadership development programs to a prospect. Depending on what their core drivers and motivators are, here's just how differently you would need to position your offering to achieve maximum excitement and attraction from that person.

- **The Aesthetic Motive** —A desire to buy things that promote life or world balance, harmony, and peace. Also, a desire to buy things that are aesthetically pleasing, comfortable (emotionally and physically), and that provide comfort or reduce effort, tension, or stress. If your prospect was driven by this dimension, you would need to make sure you accentuate all of the ways in which your solution is more elegant, will deliver more peace and harmony, reduce work hours allowing them more free time, reduce strife in the workplace, and so on.
- **The Altruistic Motive**—A drive to buy things that make life better for others, or that allow them to serve others more. If your prospect has this as their primary driver, you would need to position your offering in ways that reinforce how it will help improve the lives of the employees, build team cohesiveness, and make them a better leader for others, and so on.
- **The Economic Motive**—A motivation to buy something based on its practical value; guaranteed return on investment; or an overall value relative to price and based on comparative value to other similar things available in the marketplace. To effectively motivate a prospect with this dimension driving them, you must make clear and tangible connections to how your solution will improve monetary conditions, be more cost effective, deliver the biggest ROI, or basically increase profits for the company.
- **The Individualistic Motive**—A desire to buy things that are unique, promise to make the buyer different, or to stand apart from the rest; tailored to their specific needs (customized); or not available to the masses. Getting this prospect excited means you

need to show them how your solution will make them the hero, unique and special, or customized to just their situation rather than off-the-shelf like everyone else.

- **The Political Motive**—A motivation to buy things that will increase the buyers' stature/expertise; help make them an authority figure; increase their power, influence, reputation; or give them a competitive edge over others. Showing this prospective buyer how your solution will increase their ability to lead, help them get noticed or promoted, or give them authority or knowledge that others do not possess is the key.

- **The Regulatory Motive**—A drive to buy things that are traditional; follow a well-established process or procedure; help maintain order or bring order out of chaos; or create a routine and provide structure. Also, they prefer anything that provides security, predictability, and certainty. If you are to sell to someone with this dimension driving them, you have to demonstrate how your product is widely used; not the first movers/users; your solutions have been established; and that you have a very secure process to ensure everything is done step-by-step. Oh, and that your solution will not be disruptive and can be implemented slowly and carefully.

- **The Theoretical Motive**—A desire to buy things that deliver new knowledge, educate, teach, instruct, or provide mastery of some subject. Also, they have a desire to learn something unknown and to elevate their expertise in a given subject. Getting the high theoretical prospect can be as simple as implying "I know something you don't know." This buyer gets excited about opportunities to learn more, expand their expertise, explore unknown knowledge, and add to their mental database anything they currently don't know.

Just look at how different these motivations are. If you think of these as radio channels, sending a message on the wrong channel means your prospect never hears it, thus you fail to develop sufficient excitement or passion for what you're saying.

Remember, since you can't be all things to all people, your only rational choice is to figure out what you need to be for that one individual you are selling to. Being able to measure that person's buying motives before you recommend anything to them is the best way I've found to do that.

The Four Buying Styles (How People Buy)

Just as with understanding what motivates a prospect to buy, using a DISC profile adds to that buyer's intelligence by allowing you to understand how they like to be communicated with when you present your findings and recommendations. I call this the buyer's "buying style." It is in the buying style that you will find the information you need to effectively communicate your value to the prospect. This differs from motivations by being only about "How" they like to receive information, whereas motivations deal with "What" that motivational message is. Miss the mark here and you are putting yourself at a significant disadvantage.

For example: Imagine you are still selling leadership development to a potential client. Here's just how differently you would need to communicate with that buyer depending on their unique buying style.

- **The Dominant Buyer**—This buyer wants top-line information only. They like to move quickly, be decisive, and control the buying decision.
- **The Interactive Buyer**—This type of buyer wants a much more social interaction. They want to talk, share emotions, and enjoy the buying process.
- **The Stabilizing Buyer**—This type of buyer is the antithesis of the dominant buyer. They prefer to make the purchasing decision slowly, carefully, and with as little risk as possible.
- **The Cautious Buyer**—This type of buyer wants to make sure they buy accurately, get the most reliable and accurate product, and get all of their questions answered completely.

Buying Style Communication Tips

Selling to High D's

- Be practical and efficient (avoid theory).
- Highlight opportunities for change and adventure.
- Avoid overly emotional discussions or opinion-based arguments.
- Accentuate independence and competition.
- Challenge their idea, perhaps, but not them personally.

- Stick to the big-picture, bottom-line business at hand.
- Be quick and to the point (do not waste their time).
- Likes new, innovative things.
- Let them be in control.

Selling to High I's

- Avoid challenging them or personal conflict.
- Don't aggressively close or push.
- Be enthusiastic and express emotions.
- Let them talk!
- Highlight potential improved appearance, social standing, approval by others.
- Have fun!
- Accentuate the "newness" factor.
- Name dropping is not a bad thing here (if done tastefully, of course).

Selling to High S's

- Avoid conflict (with them or trashing anyone else, even those not present).
- Reassure and reduce risk as much as possible.
- Provide structure, step-by-step details, and security.
- Give them ample time to decide (as in days or weeks in some extreme cases).
- Accentuate your support and commitment long-term (think family).
- Be sincere, modest, and unassuming.
- Don't get too personal too fast.
- Take it slow and steady.

Selling to High C's

- Provide high levels of high-quality evidence and proof (data, facts, statistics, etc.).
- Connect to solving problems.
- Make sure zero typos, grammatical mistakes, or forgotten deliverables ever happen.

- Ensure accuracy, reliability, and dependability.
- Avoid pointing out any mistakes they may make.
- Be organized and logical.
- Be unemotional.
- Establish trust, through proof.

Who's on First?

The prospect's buying style also greatly affects how quickly they will adopt change or take a new course. Some styles love buying something new, innovative, or cutting edge. Other styles fear such things and would be pushed away from them if you tried to sell those aspects as features or a benefit.

- **Innovators** = High D's (They will buy brand new, cutting-edge solutions that have not been proven by anyone else in the market. They revel in the chance to be the first to try things.)
- **Early Adopters** = High D's and High I's (The high I's are almost as brazen as the high D's, but unlike the D's they appreciate social proof, so be sure to point out how your solution allows them to join others who are leading the way, pushing the boundaries, blazing new trails.)
- **Early Majority** = High I's and High S's (The S's come in once they know a majority exists. Not wanting to be on the front lines like the high D's and I's, the S's prefer to wait until they can be certain that the risk has been minimized by others who have tried it first.)
- **Late Majority** = High S's and High C's (High C's, if they buy in, will want to wait even longer. They will want to be even more certain, be even more assured that the solution is accurate. Allowing plenty of time for others to work the kinks out assures them of dependability.)
- **Non-Adopters** = High C's (If there is one style that may never adopt it is the High C's. They require the most proof, the most evidence, and the most "selling to" to decide to buy. They require plenty of facts, data, and proof.)

And just in case you were wondering what the odds were of running into any one of these styles out there in your marketplace, here are the percentiles from over 20 years of records:

- High D = 10 to 15 percent of the population
- High I = 25 to 35 percent of the population
- High S = 45 to 50 percent of the population
- High C = 20 to 30 percent of the population

Connection versus Speed

One last thought on buying styles. Following is an illustration designed to help you better understand how to adjust your level of connection and the speed of your sales cycle, depending on the prospect's dominant style. Figure 9.1 illustrates this relationship for you.

Connection

- When dealing with S's and I's you can connect more. Actually, doing so will improve your chances of signing their business. Just connect slowly with the High S and feel free to go a little faster with the High I.
- When dealing with high D's and C's, however, don't try to connect as much. Both styles prefer more professional relationships. Coming on too personally is to be avoided with these styles.

Speed

- When dealing with D's and I's you can move more quickly and have a shorter sales cycle. Neither requires as much evidence; both are

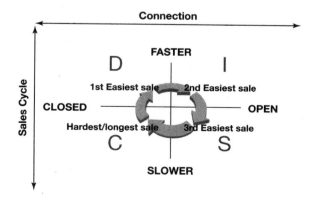

Figure 9.1   The Connection/Sales Cycle Speed Relationship

prone to making rash decisions based more on gut and intuition. High D's and I's don't like to take too long to make a decision, and hate getting caught up in the details.

■ When dealing with S's and C's, however, the exact opposite is true. You should plan on a longer sales cycle. Move too quickly and you will make these styles feel nervous. Suppress any sales training you have to get the close before you leave.

You should combine buying style and buying motives. Let's look at four examples of how you would change your approach to a prospect based on this kind of understanding. The solution is still leadership development, but the motivation and communication preferences change.

■ **Scenario #1. An economic buying motive with a High D buying style.** "This proposal will develop key leadership abilities in your leadership team, allowing them to be more effective, manage more efficiently, and in general deliver greater performance that drives more profits. Can we agree now and get moving?"

■ **Scenario #2. Same economic buying motive, but with a High S buying style.** "This proposal will drive performance and profits by creating leadership standards that all leaders meet. It has been used successfully by over 50 other corporations to create structure and order out of the chaos that was their leadership development process. Why don't I leave all of this material with you so you can review it, and then let's meet next Tuesday to discuss any questions you have."

■ **Scenario #3. An altruistic buying motive with a High C buying style.** "What I propose is to help your leaders become better developers of others. We will work to reduce existing conflicts, stem the tide of human turnover, build more cohesive teams, and improve overall morale. Here's a 10-page proposal that outlines exactly what those steps would be in detail, with supporting proof from other companies I've worked with. What other details would you like me to provide?"

■ **Scenario #4. An individual buying motive with a High I buying style.** "My proposal is to create a customized development program for you and your leaders that will target your unique needs and problems. I would like to tailor it to your specific leadership style so it would become something you drive and lead yourself, making you the primary source. We can discuss the details more if you like, but let's focus on how we can make this your leadership development program first."

See just how differently I need to position my proposal to connect with what motivates each style the most, and then how different the actual words are that I use with each? Now can you see why using profiles like these in front of the sale actually helps you make that sale to begin with? This kind of buyer intelligence is priceless.

10

Be Bold and Mighty Forces Will Come to Your Aid

Squeezing the Trigger

And now you find yourself having built the foundations for a profitable practice, chosen your target, built your weapon, and put one in the chamber. You're poised to squeeze the trigger on this thing you've created called your new consulting practice.

I'm all for aggressive action, but be wise about it. You've learned a lot of stuff and it will take a while to get it all working right. You'll make a lot of mistakes but I like to remember an old saying that goes: "Wisdom comes from good judgment. Good judgment comes from experience, and experience comes from bad judgment."

Be okay with making lots of mistakes as the more you make the wiser you become. To help you squeeze that trigger, here are the final few pieces of the puzzle I'd like to share with you.

Comfort Zones

It was the writer Dostoyevsky who wrote, "Taking a new step is what people fear most."

Getting out of your comfort zone can be a difficult thing to do for many new consultants. Unfortunately, as the new solopreneur you are, it's very likely that you will have new tasks and responsibilities that you haven't had to do before, or for a long time. Maybe you were the executive vice president of a company and it's been 20 years since you made a sales call. Perhaps you've never written and submitted articles to journals, or made a video. Whatever it is, beware the sweet siren call of your comfort zone to only do what you are most comfortable with.

I love how author Stan Dale describes it when he says, "Comfort zones are plush-lined coffins."

It is the comfort zone's job to keep you doing what you've always done. If you try to break out of these old habits and even entertain the idea of doing something different, your comfort zone starts pointing out all the negative reasons why you shouldn't do it, why it is dangerous, why you should be fearful. Your comfort zone will employ whatever tools it has at its disposal to scare you back to whatever is familiar and safe.

To be successful you are going to have to get comfortable with being uncomfortable and out of your comfort zone. Take heart, eventually your new activities too will become comfortable.

Courage to Change

For those reading this book who have long dreamt of leaving their current bonds behind, flipping the proverbial middle finger to the corporate mother ship, and starting your own consulting practice—but haven't done it yet—this one's for you.

Management theorist W. Edward Deming once said, "It is not necessary to change. Survival is not mandatory." Change requires courage, because change can be scary to some people. As it's been stated by a great many, bravery is not the act of being unafraid. It is the act of taking action *in spite of* being afraid. One very effective way to do this is to introduce an opposing and even greater fear. Since we can't get rid of fear, let's use one fear to counter another.

I tell my students, "If you make it easier to fail than to succeed, the only thing you will likely succeed at is failing." What I mean is that if on the "succeed to change" side of the scale, you have discomfort and fear, yet on the "fail to change" side you have familiarity and comfort, it's going to be a hell of a lot safer and easier to fail at changing.

The trick is to put something very significant at risk on the "fail to change" side of this equation, thus making it scarier to fail than to succeed.

There is an old, but powerful, myth that when Viking warriors would land on a foreign coast to conquer its lands, to ensure that it wasn't easier to fail in battle and return to the safety of their boats and the sea, the Vikings would burn their boats. Though a complete myth, the imagery is still very powerful. Failure wasn't much of an option. While I don't recommend risking your life to succeed, I think we can take inspiration from this legend by creating significant consequences to not changing, or not getting out of our comfort zones.

I've used this approach many times in my life, and with great success. I first learned this lesson in the military when I volunteered for a long pipeline of special operations schools. If I failed to complete any of them, or "Dropped on Request" (i.e., quit), it wasn't like I would be sent home to the relative comfort of civilian life. If I failed, my six-year contract was still completely binding. The fear of spending years doing mind numbingly boring, useless grunt work far outweighed any other fears that popped up in training, so it was easier to succeed than to fail.

Later I would quit Johnson & Johnson to start my own consulting practice. The risk of not feeding my babies or having a roof over their heads was much greater than any risks of making the start-up work, so it was easier to succeed than to fail.

Having a dream is great, and being ready for change is also important, but until you take action it is just that—a dream. And while dreams are nice, you can't get squat for them at the grocery store. You must take action.

"You can't build a reputation on what you're going to do."
—Henry Ford

If you're stuck then perhaps you can consider how you could risk something scarier than staying where you are. For some it might be risking the public embarrassment of formally telling everyone you are going to start that business you've been talking about for years. For others it might be a financial risk, as in throwing off the golden handcuffs that bind you to your current role and turning in your resignation. How will you make it easier to succeed then to fail?

Just What Is a Qualified Prospect?

As you finally start hitting the streets and actively engaging prospects, make sure they are qualified. As simple as it sounds, sometimes our passion (aka desperation) to close more business can easily lead us to find ourselves telling our story to anyone who will listen. I always start all my classes for consultants with a round of introductions. I ask my students to share with the rest of the class who they provide consulting to. I can't tell you how many times I've sat there listening to a fellow consultant answer this last part with what commonly amounts to "anyone with a pulse." Outside of the humor, the sadness of this answer shouldn't be overlooked. It is so damn important to make sure you aren't wasting your time with an unqualified lead.

Seeking to help unqualified leads will not do you or the prospect any favors. In the end you will only waste two people's time.

There's an old saying that goes, "The best thing you can tell a salesperson is 'yes.' The second best thing you can tell a salesperson is 'no'—but do it quickly." One of the biggest dangers in sales is to invest (waste) a lot of time in a sale that will never happen. Prospects that are neither qualified nor serious can suck up tons of time and still lead to nothing in the end. The "opportunity cost" of that wasted time can really add up and cost you a lot of revenue.

Instead of giving your pitch to everyone with a pulse, always try to determine whether this person is indeed a "qualified prospect" before investing too much business time.

Qualified prospects are people who:

- Have a need for what you do and admit they have it.
- Are very interested in doing something about that need.
- Have the authority and ability to hire you to help fix that need.
- And who believe (trust) in you as someone who can help.

You would be amazed at how easy it is to invest significant time with someone who fails to have all four of these qualities. Someone with only three is that much less qualified than someone with all four, and someone with only two is half as qualified. You can turn that equation around as well and have a feeling for how likely they are to become a paying client. Someone with all four qualities is twice as likely to become a client as someone with only two of them, and so on.

How tempted would you be to schedule an appointment with someone who called you to ask, "I saw your article and I love what you do. Could we schedule some time to talk about how you could help our organization?" Many of you would be very tempted. If, however, you fail to qualify this person, you could be wasting a lot of time. Before I schedule time to meet with this person I would want to at least find out what their title or position was (addressing #3 in the list above). The fact that they reached out to me pretty much checks the other boxes, but when I get together with them I would want to gauge their level of urgency more, of course.

In sales terminology the person you are really looking for is called the "economic buyer." This means they are the one who signs the check. You may have to develop relationships with lots of people who can aid or crush the final deal, but in the end the single most important person you must convince to buy is the economic buyer.

Just be careful to not give too much of your time to too many people until you can qualify them very well.

Always Deliver Superior Customer Service

When you interact with prospects or clients, one of the best ways to ensure both the success of your current interaction and future business with them is to always provide superior customer service. The following is what I consider to constitute world-class customer service:

- **The customer is always the customer.** I like to change the old phrase, "The customer is always right" a little. Many times the customer may be dead wrong, but he is still the customer, even when wrong. You can't argue with customers or embarrass them by showing them they are wrong. You must facilitate having them come up with the new (correct) idea. If what they want is so wrong that it will undermine the results, or is unethical, either figure out how to change their minds constructively or walk away from the business. Sometimes not working with them is the best service you can provide to customers.
- **Show them they are a priority.** In an attempt to serve and be responsive, sometimes we mistakenly take client calls when and where we shouldn't. Answering a client's call while you're in a loud airport, or only have "two minutes," is a mistake. It can make them feel as if you're distracted by something more important. It's better to take a voicemail, and later return the call when you are in a quiet area and have time to focus on them.
- **Always be honest, even when it hurts.** Never lie to the customer, or anyone inside the company. If you can't do something, tell them. If you screw up, tell them. If they screw up, tell them, but remember that *the customer is always the customer*.
- **Don't be afraid to apologize.** In line with the previous rule, things will go wrong. It's inevitable. I've actually heard quite a few famous people argue that to apologize is to undermine your standing. Frankly, that's just bullshit. If you screw up, apologize. There's

nothing wrong with that, and it humanizes you, which actually makes you more likeable.

- **Respect their culture.** Regardless of how you go about things, learn and respect your customer's culture. If their executives fly coach and don't take cabs, either do the same or don't charge for full reimbursement. If they wear shirts and ties, do likewise. If there are executives parking in the rear lot, park next to them. Follow their rules, their culture, and their chain of command.
- **Honor all deadlines.** One of the best ways to reinforce many of these other rules is to honor their deadlines. Not doing so makes them feel less of a priority, it isn't respectful, and can cause them to be waiting on you. When you commit to it, be sure you can meet it.
- **Respond quickly.** Whenever any request from a client comes in, react quickly. Don't let voicemails or e-mails go unanswered more than 24 hours ever. If you can't deliver what they ask, you can at least respond quickly (within an hour or less) that you received it and let them know when you can deliver it (and then honor that deadline).
- **Ask and listen.** Some consultants let their hubris get in the way and refuse to ask enough questions for fear of undermining their thought-leader status. A good consultant asks more questions than they provide answers for, and he or she requests honest feedback and accepts it positively regardless of whether it's good or bad. Listen carefully to what the clients say and show them that you heard them by feeding their statements back or incorporating them into your work visibly.
- **Don't make them chase you.** Try to anticipate needs whenever possible, and take the first step in reaching out to the client. When you can't anticipate them, make it a habit to go to them asking questions or seeking any needs they have. Except in extreme cases, learning of a need should come from a call you instigated, not from the client.
- **Respect everyone.** His Holiness the Dalai Lama was once overheard having a lengthy discussion with the housekeeper of the hotel where he was staying. He was as attentive to her as he would be to the President of the country he was there to meet. Treat the lowest-level employee you meet with the same degree of respect you would have for the highest level in the organization.

When to Squeeze the Trigger

The great US military leader General Colin Powell has a saying about when to squeeze the trigger. According to his vast experience the very best leaders take action without waiting for absolute certainty or preparedness. In other words, they move before they are as prepared as they ideally would like to be.

General Powell talks about a formula he uses, P = 40–70. Here "P" stands for Probability (of success) and the numerical values represent the percentage of information gathered. By 40 to 70 percent he means that you only have 40 to 70 percent of the information you might ideally like to have before taking action. That may mean a leader doesn't know everything he would like to know, but he moves anyway.

Yes, there's a lot to be said for proper planning (e.g., proper planning prevents piss-poor performance), but some consultants wait too long. They hold off on launching their business until they are 90 percent certain about what they are doing. This can lead to analysis paralysis, and opportunities are missed.

It will always be the case that you could prepare more, learn more, or gather more intelligence about your target market or competition. However, if you wait until you have 80 or 100 percent of the information you think you need, if you wait until you are absolutely certain you're ready, you will either never be ready or too late.

Those who succeed are those who, even knowing they aren't quite ready and still have lots of things they could improve on, squeeze that trigger and get the ball rolling.

The key lesson here is, "Take action *now!*" Don't wait until you're comfortable.

Your Launch Checklist

To help you squeeze that trigger and actually launch your new consulting practice, I've created a comprehensive checklist. All you have to do is follow the steps in the checklist in Appendix D as you complete them. Go in order from top to bottom. There are some you may choose not to do (e.g., certain marketing vehicles), but this list will help you keep track of what you've done to prepare for your launch, and what you still need to do. By the time you get to the end of the checklist, you are ready for launch!

Conclusion

Don't Lose Sight of Your Success

ENJOY THE WONDERFUL JOURNEY you are about to embark upon. It is the most wonderful ride I've ever been on, and I think most of the consultants I know would say the same. Follow the processes I've outlined for you in this guide, interact with other consultants for additional support and education, and just keep walking. Remember what I said earlier: You can't control the sale, but you can control your activity. With sufficient activity—*will* come sales. I promise!

My closing comments to you are this. After you've established your business, after you've secured several paying clients, make sure to not lose sight of your happiness.

I think it's important to point out that just because I've chosen to focus on becoming profitable doesn't mean that profits alone equal success. In my last book, *What's Your Genius*, I interviewed a lot of very successful people in multiple industries. All had reached the pinnacle of success in their chosen fields. One question I asked each interviewee was "How do you define success?" The answer I got is important because in not one single case was that answer what the general public would have expected.

Most people would have expected that answer to be "the money, fame, power I've achieved." What I heard, however, was far from that. Their definitions had nothing to do with financial success, power, control, or personal fame. In case after case, what I did hear was that their greatest success was the relationship with their family, their health and wellbeing, the feeling they received from helping others, the security they'd been able to provide their loved ones, or that they worked in their passions each and every day.

The message they send is that money can't buy happiness. I can think of lots of people who have loads of money, tons of fame, piles of achievements, and tremendous power and authority—but who are still not happy. However, all the people I know who consider themselves truly happy also consider themselves truly successful.

Therefore, it is my belief that happiness is the key ingredient in defining your success, not the result of it. I guess you could say that happiness is the DNA of success. All roads branch out from this, and all lead back to it.

Just think about it. You desire success so that you can have lots of money so that you can be financially secure—which will make you happy. You want to win the competition because you feel the need to prove yourself and have others admire you, which will make you feel better about yourself, which will make you happy. You have a desire to be in charge, on top, the big boss, to have control and prestige, to prove your worth—all of which will make you really happy.

The key is, everything is really driven by happiness, and so success at its most basic level is built on being happy, not on being successful in and of itself. The trick is figuring out what will really make you happy, because when you know this, only then do you really know what success means to you.

It's unfortunately easy to get caught up in chasing a means to an end, spending a life pursuing the trappings of success, not the happiness itself. We get easily confused about what the true objective is and many times end up sacrificing our true happiness in pursuit of some objective that was supposed to deliver our happiness in the first place. In such cases, the means actually become the end itself, and the end of our happiness as well.

Whatever you do, don't get so caught up in creating a profitable practice that you lose sight of why you wanted that practice in the first place. I've seen many a consultant work so many late hours, travel so much, and ignore those they loved so much that when they eventually reached their business dreams, there was no one left to share that success with—which made them unhappy.

The vital lesson that I would leave you with, above all others, is to make sure you're chasing happiness, not just success or the means to it.

Appendix A
Putting It All to Work
for You—A Review

NOW THAT YOU understand the five steps of this process much better, let's see what it looks like when you put it all together as a more relevant scenario for you, the business consultant. Let's watch a play called "The Sale That Wasn't a Sale."

Act 1

Scene 1—Inducing the client to come to you.

> (You're sitting in your office when the phone rings. You answer it to speak with a gentleman who says he's the president of a local manufacturing firm, and he saw one of your articles on poor sales performers and would like to talk with you about that some more. You agree to meet him for coffee the next morning. You meet each other the following morning).

You: Hi, Mr. Smith, thanks for calling and making time to meet. You said you wanted to talk about something you read in one of my articles. Which one was that again—*The Problem with Salespeople Who Suck?*

The Client: Yes, Mr. Jones, that's right.

You: Call me Johnny, please. What exactly does your company do?

The Client: Sure, no problem. We're a local manufacturing company that makes injectors for locomotive diesel engines. We do about $25 million a year. I called because I was reading your article on what drives poor sales performance and I wanted to talk with you more because we've got some really horrible salespeople right now and they're killing us!

Act 1

Scene 2—Establishing the Power Source.

(Having decided this guy sounds legitimate and has a company you might be interested in working with, and a problem you could help with, you probe to flesh the power source out a little more.)

You: Well, glad to talk about it. By "some," how many poor sales people are we talking about, and by "killing us," just how bad is it?

The Client: It's bad. We only have seven regional sales people covering the entire country. Four of them are rock solid and been around kicking butt for quite a few years. The other three are horrible, and can't sell a damn thing.

You: Let me ask you two questions. What percentage of the overall sales of your company are these three responsible for, and how much below quota are they—literally as in how many dollars have they lost you?

The Client: Collectively they represent 20 percent of total sales and I know I should probably have an exact number, but I would have to say they are roughly $5 million below quota between all of them.

Act 1

Scene 3—Advance a hypothetical cause.

(Now that you've quantified the problem, and have a good sense of what the emotional toll is, you move to the next stage of discussing possible causes.)

You: Ouch! Okay, so last question. What do you think is causing their horrible sales performance?

The Client: I don't think we do a very good job of training our salespeople. I also think that some people are just natural-born sales stars, and others are not.

You: Well, you may be right about the sales training, but I definitely agree with you on the natural-born salespeople part. In my experience I've worked with thousands of sales companies over the years and while sales training is definitely important, the much bigger piece to the puzzle is finding salespeople who have the right natural talents and strengths for selling, like aggressiveness, self-starting ability, competitiveness, assertiveness, and believe it or not emotional intelligence.

The Client: I think you're right with some of these folks as I know for a fact that two of them are nowhere near as motivated or have that same hunger I see in the other reps. Crap, so if these three we've spent a ton of money training don't have some of these natural talents, what can we do? How can we fix it? Do you provide sales training and how much do you charge?

Act 1

Scene 4—Recommend the diagnostic profile.

(Sitting pretty with power source and agreement from your prospect on the possible cause of the solution, you shut down your desire to jump straight to selling your sales profiling services, and stick to the plan. You make sure you know the problem, not just guess at it.)

You: Oh, there's a whole lot we could do, but before I could talk about how to fix that problem of sucking sales, and even think about price, I'd need to know if I'm right and the reason you are down $5 million in sales is because these kinds of hallmark sales strengths are damn near absent from some of your salespeople, or what. Before we start talking solution, I'd like to make sure I'm right and actually measure these traits in your sales staff. Why guess when we can know, right?

The Client: So what's that going to cost me?

You: At this point, it's not going to cost you a dime because until I know what the real cause of the problem is, I don't know if there's anything I can do to help and what that would cost. Don't get me wrong. I'm not avoiding your question. It's just way too early to talk steps or price until we see what's really driving the poor performance, which could be different for each person. Trust me, when I know what the problem is I will be more than glad to propose some solutions and even more glad to quote you a big fat consulting fee for fixing it. Don't worry about that.

The Client: Oh, I don't doubt that. So what's the next step?

You: I'd like to confirm this diagnosis, if you will, by having your entire sales team, all seven, complete a free sales diagnostic profile. This way I can compare poor sales performers with top folks, to see what differences there are. The profile takes about 15 minutes to complete online, is so valid it will scare you, and it measures all the key sales traits I need to see in order to understand why they aren't selling. Once I get those back, let's schedule a short meeting to go over the results and I'll tell you what I found. All I need you to do is have your admin send each of the reps a link I will provide you when I get back to the office. Then we'll talk. Does that work for you?

The Client: Hey, if it doesn't cost me anything, but could help me figure out why I've lost $5 million, why not! When do you want to meet again to go over the results?

You: Well, I can meet this coming Friday if you can get them to complete the instrument by Thursday evening.

The Client: Well shit, half of them aren't busy doing any selling anyway so don't worry about that. I can promise you they will complete it by then.

Act 1

The Finale—Negotiate the appropriate solution.

(The sales reps complete the DISC Index profile, you review the results, and sure enough find some really low scores in the three poor performers, and notice some stark differences between top and bottom performers as well. Calling the President and confirming your meeting for Friday, you tease him a little by stating, "Oh, and I definitely see some things that could be causing the problem." You arrive for your meeting and walk into the President's office.)

You: Hi, Mr. Smith, how has your week been?

The Client: It sucked. We're still losing sales, what can you tell me? I'm dying here!

You: Here are the profiles of your sales team. Even though there's a ton of information in there, that's all stuff I would use in training or coaching, so there's way too much to go over in the time we have here. That doesn't matter though, because the point of this meeting is to see if we were right or not, and if there is a big natural talent gap between the best and the worst. And there definitely is!

The Client: Okay, again you're killing me here. What's the difference specifically?

You: Let's look at Frank's page four, which summarizes the core talents. See this bar, the Decisiveness one? Frank's got a 15, which means he can't make a decision to save his life. Your top four sales people all have above an 85 here. Susan and Gunther have slightly higher levels of Decisiveness than Frank, but still way below your four rock stars. Also, see how Frank and Susan are super high in this dimension called Stability? Most great salespeople are actually low here, which makes them love fast-paced, dynamic environments where everything is constantly moving and exciting. Your top sales guys have low scores here too, meaning they love chaotic, seat-of-the-pants, sales environments. Frank and Susan, on the other hand, hate that kind of pace. They like to take everything very slowly, have lots of time to think things through and not be pushed or rushed to respond. In your sales do you find it's vital to be able to think on your feet and handle whatever is thrown at you, or are your sales much slower paced, calm and nonaggressive?

The Client: Our sales are anything but slow or nonaggressive. It's like combat out there some days, and our folks have got to be able to spin on a dime and completely change course because our customers or suppliers are constantly throwing curve balls.

You: Yeah, all three of your low performers will basically suck at handling that kind of environment. Look, overall there are several other things like resistance to aggressively close, being too empathetic, and a lack of a high sense of urgency in all three bottom folks, yet none of those problems exist in your top performers. I'm about as confident as I get that these traits are completely undermining their ability to effectively sell your products to your customers.

The Client: So what do we do about it? Can you train them to get better in these areas, or should I just fire them?

You: Here's what I've done with other clients in similar situations, and it's worked very well. First there is some training that I can provide that will help each of these salespeople leverage what natural talents they do have. They don't all need to be complete copies, or exactly the same. I can help them learn those weaknesses better as well, so they won't let them get in the way as much. Outside of that, the real key is to make sure that when you do hire new salespeople for whatever reason, you identify these traits early on so you're not left trying to retrofit someone who wasn't a great fit in the first place. I recommend you focus on the training part first, and I would include all seven salespeople because they all have some short or long list of strengths and weaknesses that they could improve on. Once we get done with that, let's discuss hiring when you're ready. My training program costs $5,000 per head, so you'd be looking at $35,000 total, payable in three equal payments.

The Client: Damn, that's kind of expensive!

You: I appreciate that it's expensive. I also think it's a hell of a good deal when you consider it's only about 0.7 percent of the sales you've already lost this year, and we need to get this fixed before you lose that much again next year.

The Client: Point well taken. Okay, so how do we start?

The end—or just the *actual* beginning . . .

Appendix B
The EBM Guide

How to Get Started on an EBM Campaign

WHILE STARTING AN EBM program may sound a little intimidating at first, in reality it's incredibly simple (and that's not hyperbole). Let me show you how simple it is. Take a minute to answer the following questions:

- Would you consider yourself expert enough in one single topic to speak authoritatively to a group of friends at dinner? Yes   No
- What would that topic be? _____
- Would this topic be of compelling interest to a significant portion of your target market? Yes   No
- Could you fill three notebook pages with notes—straight out of your head, right now—on this topic (e.g., key points, causes, trends, common mistakes, tips and developmental ideas)? Yes   No

That's it! If you answered yes to the questions above (and identified a topic) then you have everything you need to kick off an EBM program and start positioning yourself as the expert you are . . . today.

243

Action Steps:

1. **Market**—Select your **market** (who needs your expertise—make it "niched"): _____

   _____

   _____

2. **Message**—Select your **topic** (what can you speak as an expert on, and what does your target market want to learn more about? *Hint: make the topic relevant to a significant problem in the chosen market*):

   _____

   _____

   _____

3. **Vehicle**—Select your **medium** (where will your message be seen?—the more the merrier):
   a. Newspaper article
   b. Write a book (full length or e-book)
   c. Your newsletter
   d. Case study/white paper
   e. Journal article
   f. Website (blog, videos, podcasts)
   g. Online article submission sites
   h. Social media (Twitter, Facebook, LinkedIn)
   i. Teleseminar
   j. Webinar
   k. Live seminar/speaking (free or fee)
      Choose your timeframe:
      i. Ready to roll: _____ / _____
      ii. Start marketing the event: _____ / _____
         (live, virtual, *or* written, you should build excitement for the event/publication in advance)
      iii. Actual launch date: _____ / _____

4. **Advertise** your program (how will they know to come/read/watch):
   a. E-mail invite (broadcast e-mails to your opt-in network)
   b. Partners
   c. Marketing affiliates (others who can advertise in their networks):

      _____

      _____

      _____

    i. Chambers of Commerce (geographically close):

_____

_____

_____

    ii. Associations (who has members hungry for your content?):

_____

_____

_____

  d. Website promotions

  e. Social media (Twitter, Facebook, LinkedIn, etc.)

5. **Execute**—you have to actually DO IT!
6. **Repeat** (go back to step 1 and pick a new topic, new market, new vehicle).

Remember, EBM is about EDUCATING . . . prolifically!

Diagnostic Sales Cheat Sheet

Make sure to follow each step in the process and use this guide to ensure you get the key pieces of each step along the way.

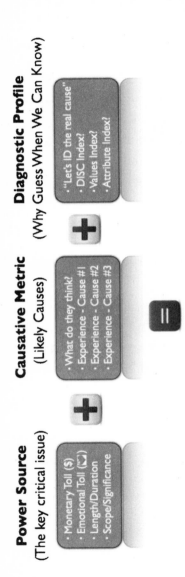

Power Source
(The key critical issue)

- Monetary Toll ($)
- Emotional Toll (☹)
- Length/Duration
- Scope/Significance

Causative Metric
(Likely Causes)

- What do they think?
- Experience – Cause #1
- Experience – Cause #2
- Experience – Cause #3

Diagnostic Profile
(Why Guess When We Can Know)

- "Let's ID the real cause"
- DISC Index?
- Values Index?
- Attribute Index?

The Custom Solution
(The Individualized Solution Based on the Findings of the Diagnostic Profiling)

- Debrief the profile – short "sales" orientation debrief to highlight specific causes only
- Connect the Dots between findings and the actual problem (get their buy-in)
- Respond to buy-sign questions (e.g., "How do we fix that")
- Provide a call to action. You MUST make a recommendation!

Figure B.1 Diagnostic Sales Cheat Sheet

Appendix C
Press Release
Template

Insert your company logo here

FOR IMMEDIATE RELEASE

Contact: John Dough
Phone: 123-456-7891
Email: jdough@playdoe.com

MAIN TITLE HERE. ALWAYS IN ALL CAP AND BOLD.
Subtitle here (Upper and Lower case, but bold as well.

Body goes here. Lead needs to cover the whole story assuming they read nothing else. Copy, copy, copy, copy, copy, copy, copy.

Second paragraph, expand Who, How, What, Where, When and Why. copy, copy, copy, copy, copy, copy. copy, copy, copy, copy, copy, copy. copy, copy, copy, copy, copy, copy. copy, copy, copy, copy, copy, copy. copy, copy, copy, copy. copy, copy, copy, copy, copy, copy. copy, copy, copy, copy, copy, copy. copy, copy, copy, copy, copy, copy. copy, copy, copy, copy, copy, copy.

Final paragraph. Wrap it up.

###

To speak with John Dough contact him at (insert phone number, email address, mailing address).

Appendix D
Launch Cheat Sheet

Launch Checklist

USE THE CHECKLIST below to keep track of the steps you've taken as you build your new practice, prepare for going to market, kick off your marketing activities, and head out the door to land your very first client. Hey, if it was easy, everyone would be making fat six-figures working in their pajamas.

Chapter 2—Building a Foundation

1. ☐ Choose my company name: _____
2. Choose my business structure: _____
   - ☐ Sole proprietorship
   - ☐ S Corporation
   - ☐ LLC
   - ☐ C Corporation
   - ☐ Other: _____

3. Get business insurance:
   - ☐ Property
   - ☐ Liability
   - ☐ Other: _____

4. Create business plan (start now—finalize at end of book):
   - ☐ Did it myself
   - ☐ Used One Page Business Plan

5. Create my brand:
   - ☐ Rough draft mission statement: _____
     _____

   - ☐ Design brand logo/image
     Protect my brand:
     - ☐ LegalZoom (or)
     - ☐ US Patent & Trademark Office

6. Stock up on supplies:
   - ☐ Computer
   - ☐ Printer/Scanner/Copier
   - ☐ Business Cards
   - ☐ E-mail
   - ☐ Letterhead & Envelopes
     Brochures:
     - ☐ Digital (and/or)
     - ☐ Physical
     Phone line:
     - ☐ Voicemail
     - ☐ Conferencing capability
     - ☐ Answering service
   - ☐ Headshot photos
   - ☐ Webinar service

7. Establish my Internet presence:
   - ☐ Build website (and link to my social media outlets)
     Open social media accounts:
     - ☐ LinkedIn
     - ☐ Facebook
     - ☐ YouTube
     - ☐ Twitter

☐ Set up my blog:
    ☐ Submit it to all blog registry sites

8. ☐ Open my merchant services banking account
9. Open my office:
    ☐ Home-based (or)
    ☐ Rent office space
10. Get software programs:
    ☐ Accounting software
    ☐ Scheduling/Calendar software
    ☐ Project management software
    ☐ CRM software
11. Define my role:
    ☐ Complete the strengths profile:
      i. Top 5 greatest strengths: _____

      _____
      _____
      _____
      _____

      ii. Top 5 greatest weaknesses: _____

      _____
      _____
      _____
      _____

    ☐ Complete the CEO Bucket List exercise
    ☐ Outsourcing list:
      i. Duties & name/s to outsource to: _____

      _____
      _____

Chapter 3—The Money Side

12. ☐ Determine my true hourly rate: $ _____
13. Choose my preferred fee structures (as many as I like):
    ☐ Hourly: $ _____
    ☐ Per Diem: $ _____
    ☐ Retainer-based (TBD—case by case)

☐ Project-based (TBD—case by case)
Contingency:
☐ Set reward fee (TBD—case by case)
☐ Set percentage fee (TBD—case by case)
☐ Equity-based (TBD—case by case)

Chapter 5—Choose Your Target Audience

14. Choose my target audience:
☐ Niche #1:
    i. Industry: _____
    ii. Ideal prospect title:_____
☐ Niche #2:
    i. Industry: _____
    ii. Ideal prospect title:_____
☐ Niche #3:
    i. Industry: _____
    ii. Ideal prospect title:_____
15. ☐ Fill my tool bag (what I will sell):_____
    #1: _____
    #2: _____
    #3: _____
    #4: _____
    #5: _____
    #6: _____
    #7: _____
    #8: _____
    #9: _____
    #10: _____
16. ☐ Write my Unique Value Proposition: _____
    _____
    _____
17. ☐ Add my UVP to website and final mission statement

Chapter 6—Seek Only to Give

18. ☐ Create my first EBM article

19. Select your marketing vehicles:
  a. ☐ Articles:
    ☐ Title: _____
    ☐ Submitted to online sites
    ☐ Submitted to associations
    ☐ Linked to my social media outlets
  b. ☐ Blog:
    ☐ Title: (Same as above since I'm repurposing)
    ☐ Submitted to online blog sites
    ☐ Submitted to associations
    ☐ Linked to my social media outlets
  c. ☐ Lecture:
    ☐ Venue: _____
    ☐ Date: _____
    ☐ Who am I inviting: _____
    ☐ Associations targeted
    ☐ Free or ☐ Fee: $_____
  d. ☐ PowerPoint Presentation:
    ☐ Title: (same as above since I'm repurposing)
    ☐ Submitted to online presentation sites
    ☐ Linked to my social media outlets
  e. ☐ Video:
    ☐ Title: (Same as above)
    ☐ Submitted to online video sites
    ☐ Posted to my YouTube account
    ☐ Linked to my social media sites
  f. ☐ Podcast:
    ☐ Title: (same as above)
      Bought:
    ☐ Audacity
    ☐ Encoder
    ☐ Host
    ☐ Submitted to podcast sites
    ☐ Linked to my social media sites
  g. ☐ Workshop:
    ☐ Title: _____
    ☐ Virtual or ☐ Live
    ☐ Venue: _____

☐ Invited attendees/Promoted
☐ Registration link on my website
☐ Handouts ready
h. ☐ Book:
  ☐ Title: _____
  ☐ Sales page on my website
  ☐ Sample chapters on sales page
  ☐ Traditional publisher route:
    i. Found literary agent: _____
    ii. Submit proposals to publishers
  ☐ Self-publishing route?
    ☐ Selected publisher: _____
i. ☐ Drip campaign:
  ☐ Autoresponder: _____
  ☐ Campaign e-mails written
  ☐ Squeeze page created
  ☐ Connected to article/blog/video and running
j. ☐ Partners:
  1st: _____
  2nd: _____
  3rd: _____
  4th: _____
k. ☐ Networking:
  i. Locations/Groups: _____
    _____
    _____
    _____
    _____
    _____
  ii. Number of times: per week_____per month_____
l. ☐ Research:
  i. Industry: _____
  ii. Topic/Power Source: _____
  iii. Research Partner/PhD: _____
    _____
m. ☐ Press release:
  ☐ Write my press release
  ☐ Submit it to entire list of press outlets

n. ☐ Social media:
    ☐ Post link to all previous vehicles
    ☐ Daily/Weekly Twitter
    ☐ Daily/Weekly Facebook
    ☐ Daily/Weekly LinkedIn

Chapter 7—Diagnostic Selling

20. Select your diagnostic profile:
    ☐ Provider: _____
    ☐ Profile name: _____
    ☐ Practiced on _____ people
    Trained/Certified:
      ☐ Yes
      ☐ No
21. ☐ LAUNCH!!! If you haven't already, you've got everything you need so get out there and get your first paying client!
22. Go back to #18 in this checklist; create a new EBM article and Repeat, Repeat, Repeat.

About the Author

Jay Niblick is the founder and CEO of Innermetrix Incorporated, a professional consulting and technology firm with offices on five continents specializing in helping professional business consultants and coaches build and grow a profitable consulting practice (www .innermetrix.com).

Jay is also cofounder and Chief Science Advisor to the online coaching company InnerTalent, and founder and managing partner at Consultant Growth Systems.

He holds multiple technology patents, trademarks, and copyrights on diagnostic instruments and consultative methodologies relating to identifying and maximizing human talent, and is the bestselling author of the *Attribute Index* diagnostic profile (over 600,000 copies sold worldwide), and *What's Your Genius—How the Best Think for Success* (foreword by Anthony Robbins).

He has keynoted and lectured to organizations around the world in the areas of strategic management, peak performance, executive coaching, leadership development, and organizational development. Over 1,750 independent management consultants have paid to attend one of Jay's international workshops or certification programs delivering best practices on how to build a successful consulting practice and increase profitability.

Jay also sits as an officer on the Board of Directors at the Robert S. Hartman Institute (a scholarly project at the University of Tennessee in the United States dedicated to the study of human nature, value, and decision making).

Prior to consulting, Jay worked in the surgical sales industry for Johnson & Johnson. Before that he trained and served in the Special Operations communities of the US Navy and US Marine Corps during Desert Storm.

He resides in greater Philadelphia, Pennsylvania, with his wife and three sons.

Index

M

Mac *vs.* PC computers, 31
Macy's, 23
management consulting
    about, 7–9
    business markets for, 14–15
    choosing as career, 1–3, 7–8
    consulting firm types, 7
    consulting purpose hierarchy,
        9–12
    "die-chotomy" of independent
        consulting, 175–176
    DTS model for, 12, 102–108
    experience needed for, 16–17
    global consulting revenues, 15
    hiring consultants, reasons for,
        9
    independent effort and success
        in, 16, 223–225, 231–233
    industry trends in, 14–15
    low cost of business, 30–31, 41
    practice mind-sets for, 12–14
    risks of independent consulting,
        15–16
    roles and criteria for
        consultants, 7–12
    satisfaction of consultants, 173
marketing
    education-based marketing
        (EBM), 113–119, 143,
        150–152, 157, 243–246
    effective marketing, 113
    interruption-based marketing,
        113–114
    nonstarters in, 169–170
    sales-based marketing, 113–114
marketing materials
    brochures and materials, 34–36

business cards, 32–33
    logos and images for, 29, 33,
        145
    online printing services for, 32,
        34, 36
    professional bios, 44, 130
    stock headshots, 38–40
    See also branding; website
        development
Marketing News, 115
marketing vehicles
    about, 118–119, 170
    article marketing, 130–131
    audio podcast marketing,
        139–142
    book marketing, 145–149
    brochure marketing, 34–36
    drip or e-mail marketing,
        149–153
    launch checklist for, 252–254
    lecture/seminar marketing,
        131–133
    network-based marketing,
        156–159
    partnership marketing,
        155–156
    presentation marketing,
        136–137
    press release marketing,
        162–168, 247
    referral marketing, 153–155
    research-based marketing,
        159–162
    social media marketing, 121–123
    video marketing, 137–139
    webinar marketing, 133–136
    website marketing, 119–121
    workshop marketing, 142–145